Creative Living London

Creative Living London

Photographs by Ingrid Rasmussen

Emily Wheeler

West

This book is dedicated to Rowie,
a true creative.

On the cover *Front* A rich, dark colour scheme adds to the look of elegant sophistication in Graham and Jo Atkins-Hughes' Victorian terraced house in Hackney. *Back, clockwise from top left* Marc Newson and Charlotte Stockdale's warehouse conversion in Victoria; Adriana Natcheva's modern flat in Kensington; a bright and cheerful entrance to a Georgian house in Islington; a groovy, geometric rug adds a contemporary feel to Marianne Cotterill's elegant house in Brondesbury; the crisp, modern exterior of a revamped pianola factory in Kentish Town; vintage suitcases make for an unusual storage solution at a period cottage in Stockwell.

Previous pages In Spitalfields, a historic area of East London, the neighbourhood's period brick buildings share a street corner with the glass-and-steel skyscrapers of the modern city.

First published in the United Kingdom in 2013
by Thames & Hudson Ltd, 181A High Holborn,
London WC1V 7QX

Creative Living London © 2013
Thames & Hudson Ltd, London
Text © 2013 Emily Wheeler
Photographs © 2013 Ingrid Rasmussen (ingridrasmussen.com)

Designed by This-Side (this-side.co.uk)

British Library Cataloguing-in-Publication Data
A catalogue record for this book is available from the British Library

ISBN 978-0-500-51697-3

Printed and bound in China by C & C Offset Printing Co. Ltd.

To find out about all our publications, please visit
www.thamesandhudson.com. There you can subscribe to
our e-newsletter, browse or download our current catalogue,
and buy any titles that are in print.

East

Introduction

London's creative credentials are the envy of the world, and the uniquely quirky, eccentric style and independent spirit of its residents have ensured the city's reputation as the capital of edgy cool. With its renowned fashion and art colleges, a thriving music industry and internationally respected arts institutions, London is home to some of the world's most prominent artists, stylists and designers. How these energetic, talented people turn their creative vision into homes that are beautiful to look at and inspiring to live in is the theme of this book.

Despite its status as a very modern city, much of London's housing stock is centuries old. The transformation of these historic, sometimes industrial spaces into contemporary, design-savvy spaces that cleverly combine old and new (a key trend in London interiors) is a challenge facing today's city dwellers. One of these homes belongs to artistic producer Michael Smythe (p. 200), who lives in a Victorian warehouse in the East London neighbourhood of Shoreditch. His pared-back style respects the integrity of the building's working past, even down to retaining the hundreds of nails in the original floorboards, a reminder of the craftsmen of 120 years ago. In nearby Spitalfields, architect Chris Dyson (p. 180) has made it his mission to restore the area's eighteenth-century houses, which once belonged to immigrant Huguenot silkweavers, but have been abandoned and left to decay in recent decades. After a sympathetic, ten-year restoration, one of these houses is now Chris's own home (another, a few doors down, serves as his office) and, like Michael's studio, is a tribute to craftsmen past and present.

Finding inspiration in the modern city is also key. Jeweller Mawi Keivom (p. 208), who lives with her husband Tim in a Victorian villa in Dalston, a trendy corner of Hackney, has found the numerous vintage shops in and around Dalston and nearby London Fields an invaluable resource. With its Victorian and Georgian terraces, large park and picturesque canal, overlooked by converted warehouses, the area's mix of independent bookstores, coffee shops, pubs and local market attracts droves of creative freelancers, fashion bloggers and street artists, who use the local buildings and shopfronts as canvases for their work. Interior designer Graham Judkins (p. 86) was lucky enough to build up an impressive collection of street art (including a number of works by Banksy) while living in the area – a collection that now adorns the walls of his Maida Vale flat on the other side of the city.

With a continually evolving mix of people and styles to draw creative inspiration from, London interiors are often intensely personal spaces. In Islington, a northerly neighbourhood that straddles the east–west divide, artists Annie Morris and Idris Khan (p. 274) turned their Georgian townhouse into a truly bespoke home inspired by Charleston, Vanessa Bell's farmhouse in East Sussex, where Bell, Duncan Grant and the rest of the Bloomsbury set spent their days, and filled it with their own sculptures, paintings and photographs. And over in Hampstead, the home of artist Rory Dobner (p. 136) is also a reflection of his creative spirit. Rory's meticulous, often humorous inked drawings are a little bit rock 'n' roll, a little bit historical parody, and feature heavily in the Victorian maisonette that he shares with his wife and two young sons.

Colour features strongly in the home of make-up artist Lisa Eldridge and her husband Robin Derrick (p. 36), creative director of British

Vogue. Their flat, located in a converted piano factory in Camden, just down the road from Hampstead, has been revamped by a palette of deep purples, blues, reds and pinks into a stylish family home. To the west in Willesden, textile designer Margo Selby (p. 146) has also used a riot of colour and pattern to transform the house she grew up in into the ideal environment in which to try out her designs. A bus ride south of Willesden is Notting Hill, the home of Portobello Road market and the Notting Hill Carnival, as well as jeweller Pippa Small (p. 166). Her home, a two-bedroom modern flat in an area characterized by grand Georgian terraces, is a kaleidoscope of colour that gives visitors the feeling of, as she puts it, 'floating on the inside of a rainbow'.

With more and more people choosing to work from home, the need to separate work space from family life presents unique challenges when it comes to the design of one's home. In her flat, a Victorian conversion in Dalston, fashion designer Ally Capellino (p. 296) sketches her designs at a desk in the living room or at the huge kitchen table, which in its former life was a shop counter at one of her stores. Interior designer Jo Berryman (p. 108) has given over a whole floor of her house in Hampstead to her design studio, meeting clients in her sitting room and working out designs on a table designed by Eero Saarinen. Artist Martin Firrell (p. 46), the only one of our homeowners to live in central London, sits in the same spot at his dining table every day, inspired by the views over Soho from his window and rarely allowing visitors to intrude upon the peace and tranquillity of his private space. However these creatives choose to work, it is the space they have created around them at home that continues to inspire.

West

Opposite A row of terraced houses in bright pastel colours in Camden.

Following pages London's rich history is reflected in its architecture, both domestic and commercial, including a shopfront for Alice's Antiques in Portobello Road.

Pages 14–15 Just a stone's throw from Covent Garden is Henrietta Street, lined with grand stucco façades.

Stretching from Soho at its bustling heart all the way out to leafy, well-heeled Richmond, West London is where the royal parks, theatres, shops and museums that the city is known for can be found. Traditionally London's wealthier half, businessmen, celebrities and royalty have all made their homes here, avoiding its grimier neighbour to the east. West London is formed of a series of village-like areas, from the winding, cobbled streets of Hampstead in the north, which has been home to successive waves of artists and writers, and a large Jewish community that has been established here for generations, to Clapham and Battersea, south of the river, bounded by Northcote Road and its coffee shops and restaurants on one side and the looming hulk of Battersea Power Station on the other. Down the hill from Hampstead is Camden, which boasts a huge market that is popular with students and is an epicentre of alternative culture, and further south is Regent's Park, with its grand Regency terraces by John Nash, the home of the London Zoo. To the west, Notting Hill's rows of Georgian terraces are now the houses of the fabulously rich, but the area was formerly associated with poverty and was the scene of great social change in the 1970s. Today its local market in Portobello Road is known the world over, famous for its hundreds of vintage and antiques stalls. And there are many more: Brondesbury, Kensington, Victoria, Stockwell, Maida Vale, each with its own distinctive character. The East End may have the edge in hipster desirability, but West London is every bit as diverse, varied and community orientated as its eastern neighbour.

HENRIETTA
STREET WC2

CITY OF WESTMINSTER

Architect
Studio flat | Kensington

Opposite A black glass coffee table by Willy Rizzo is the focal point in the double-height living room. Above is a Venetian chandelier.

Below One of the sliding doors opens onto a corridor, leading to a small bathroom; another opens to reveal a wardrobe, transforming the space into a dressing room. On the mezzanine level, the bedroom is a simple space with a luxurious leather floor.

Adriana Natcheva, a partner at Groves Natcheva architectural practice, challenged all the rules about decorating small spaces when she refurbished her studio flat. Having fallen in love with the look of the building, a former stable block just a stone's throw from Kensington Gardens, Adriana bought the flat in 2008 and set about creating a warm, comfortable home by using natural materials with dark tones, such as wood and leather, and ceramic tiles, along with the clever use of space that one would expect from a top architect. 'I liked the external environment and the views,' she says. 'I also liked the volume of the space, and knew that I could work with it to create something good. All the fundamentals were there.'

When Adriana first moved into the flat, it was split into several different rooms with low ceilings and only one north-facing window. She gutted the whole space, tearing down the partition walls and leaving only a shell, and added windows at the back to bring in light from the south, along with a mezzanine level above the dining area to contain the bedroom. The kitchen and bar, dressing room and a hallway leading to the bathroom were concealed behind sleek sliding doors, which can be open or shut to instantly transform the room. On the mezzanine level, her bedroom appears to float above the dining space, while a library, accessed by ladder, is tucked into the space above the sliding doors. Adriana kept the space cohesive by using the same materials throughout, including African ebony for the floors

and staircase, mahogany for the windows and shutters, black lacquer for the sliding doors and kitchen, and white plaster for the walls. 'I wanted the space to have a single volume, like a boat,' she says, 'which would contain all the different elements of a house.'

Adriana's design philosophy for her professional practice is manifested in her designs for her own home. 'If there is a common thread in my work it is the belief that the spaces we live in, and the objects we interact with, should be beautiful, and this beauty we find in the human form,' she explains. 'So we look to humanize our work, and anything that we can't make beautiful, we hide out of view.' Everything in the flat has been chosen with beauty in mind, including Venini chandeliers, designed at the time when Carlo Scarpa was artistic director at the Murano glass house, and a glass coffee table by Willy Rizzo in the main living space. Beneath the mezzanine platform, a mahogany table from Sweden, surrounded by mahogany and leather chairs, defines the dining area. When it comes to her clients, Adriana believes that their homes should be a reflection of their personalities – and applies the same principle to her own home.

'Since this is my space, it reflects who I am and what is beautiful to me,' she says. 'I live in one room, which has many guises, just like a person has many moods. I love every one of them.'

Above A Swedish table and chairs from the 1950s add warmth to the dining room. The stairs behind lead up to the mezzanine-level bedroom.

Opposite Black-lacquered doors slide open to reveal an elegant kitchen with a black marble worktop.

Above and right The warm tones of the floors and shutters provide a sophisticated backdrop to the vintage furnishings and luxurious fabrics. Below the library, a hidden wardrobe is revealed.

Opposite A vintage Eames recliner sits in the corner of the sitting room, beneath the mezzanine.

Marianne Cotterill

Stylist
Victorian house | Brondesbury

Above The beautiful stained glass in the front door and in the window on the first-floor landing is one of the house's many original features.

Opposite An elegant antique French sofa, covered in silk, is complemented by a contemporary rug from The Rug Company.

Stylist Marianne Cotterill's five-storey Victorian house in Brondesbury, a genteel neighbourhood of Kilburn, just west of West Hampstead, encapsulates her eccentrically English sense of style. Highly decorative, glamorous and bohemian, the house is filled with furniture and objets d'art that she has collected on her travels or during her long career as one of the UK's top interior stylists. The result is a quirky mix of old and new, classic and kitsch, delicate and bold.

Marianne trained in textiles at the University of Birmingham and interior design at the Chelsea School of Art, but dropped out after finding the course too narrow and technical for her creative personality. The move led to fashion styling for magazines such as *Elle* and *Marie Claire*, until she and her husband Terry began to think about starting a family. The couple were living in a beautiful Georgian terraced house in Hackney at the time, and Marianne found success in renting out the house as a location for editorial, film and television shoots. Such was her creative flair that offers for work as an interiors stylist were soon flooding in, and she now works for an impressive list of commercial and private clients, styling everything from villas in Ibiza to houses in London's Fitzrovia.

Despite its huge success as a location, the Hackney house presented problems for the couple, which eventually forced them to move. In the late 1980s and early 1990s, the East End had not yet transformed into the fashionable and desirable place to live it was to become, and Marianne and Terry suffered numerous burglaries. It was after their car had been stolen and left across town in Brondesbury Park that the couple found both their new home and their abandoned car, which had been left outside of it. The house had been in the same family for generations, remaining untouched for years, and was one of the few in the area that had not been converted into flats. 'The kids called it the psycho house, because there was no sign of life and everything about it was grey,' remembers Marianne. 'An old lady had been living here for sixty years, and it had always been in her family, so it was still quite grand inside.' Marianne and Terry made an offer on the spot, and the house was theirs.

The house's original features were intact, including the wallpaper in the top-floor bedrooms. 'It was lovely, but I couldn't expect the kids to live with Victorian shabbiness, so we redecorated everywhere, rewired, re-plumbed and removed a wall on the lower ground floor to make a bigger kitchen.' The house's six bedrooms, three bathrooms, three reception rooms, conservatory and family kitchen now provide endless space for Marianne to try out ideas, and she is constantly bringing back new pieces of furniture, which the house easily absorbs. With an attic and basement full of props, she is continually changing things around and repainting the walls in new colours.

Marianne's children have not always been such huge fans of her eclectic bohemian style, preferring their rooms to be modern and comfortable. Now they are grown up, she finds they are more appreciative of her innate talent for unusual combinations of colour and pattern, and her gift for creating beautiful interiors. 'It was really only when Topshop photographed their latest campaign here one year that the kids realized I might have some idea what I was doing,' Marianne laughs. 'Now they love it.'

Opposite The original floor tiles in the kitchen and dining room have been restored, and are now topped by Eero Saarinen's 'Tulip' dining table and chairs.

Below A range cooker sits at the heart of the light and airy marble white kitchen, with accents of pink and blue for a pretty, vintage feel.

Following pages The huge canvas above the bed was a prop from a magazine shoot. A brightly patterned rug from The Rug Company injects colour into the otherwise monochromatic bedroom.

Right and below Marianne constantly trawls antiques fairs and flea markets to source items for the house or for her styling work.

Opposite The house's period details form an elegant counterpoint to Marianne's eclectic collection of glamorous lamps and vintage finds.

'I'm very undisciplined at home because I like beautiful things,' says Marianne. 'I bring them back regardless, never thinking about where I'm going to put them. I love sofas, and I now have twenty-two!'

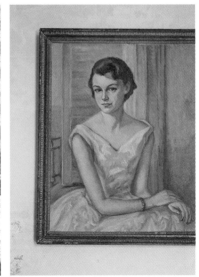

Make-up artist & creative director
Converted piano factory | Camden

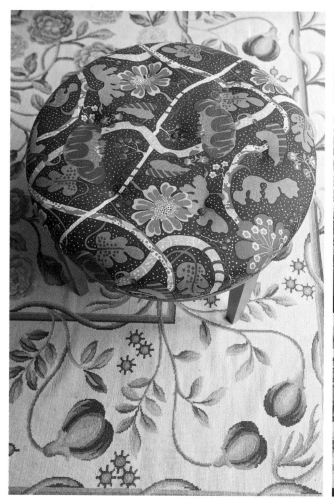

When internationally renowned make-up artist Lisa Eldridge and her husband Robin Derrick, creative director of British *Vogue*, were looking for a new home in the city, they saw numerous Victorian and Georgian terraced houses, but couldn't help feeling that they were all too small and dark for both them and their two teenage sons. But when they walked through the door of a converted piano factory in Camden, the couple immediately knew they wanted to live there and snapped it up on the spot. 'We both said this is a great space, we could have brilliant parties here, and that was it!' recalls Lisa. 'It had a really nice feel. It felt like a happy place, and had a relaxed vibe. It was out of our comfort zone, in a good way, and we knew we could make it work.'

Lisa and Robin researched the history of the building, finding it mentioned in a book about the area, which featured drawings from 1840 when it was built, and discovered that it was owned by the biggest importer of pianos at the time. The building was later used as the offices of a number of architectural firms, before being converted into a residential space

Above Colour and pattern were important to Lisa when designing her home. Samples pinned to the family's noticeboard provide further inspiration.

Opposite A bright sofa by Josef Frank at Svenskt Tenn is the focal point of the living area. Behind it on the wall is the couple's collection of art and fashion photography prints.

the year before Lisa and Robin found it. 'Although we liked the layout, we didn't like any of the finishes,' Lisa says. 'It felt more like an office, with fluorescent strip lights and masses of larch cladding on the walls. It was more like an Austin Powers ski lodge, a playboy palace, rather than a family home!' After living in the flat for a while, the couple gradually transformed it by introducing sleek finishes, sophisticated lighting, vintage furniture and plenty of brightly coloured textiles.

On the first floor, they replaced the kitchen units, removed the strip lighting and added a black vinyl floor, and had a new top made for the kitchen table out of warm natural oak, as well as re-upholstering the banquette seating in the dining nook. 'I spent ages looking at modern fabrics, but it looked too much like a boutique hotel, too try-hard,' says Lisa. 'Then I found a little piece of *toile de joie*, and I knew I needed to look at

Above The original beams are a reminder of the building's industrial history. Bright textiles and vintage finds keep the space cosy and warm.

Above Furnishings in bright colours have been used throughout the flat to make this a fun family home.

Following pages The couple designed the berry-coloured cabinets, which stretch from the kitchen into the sitting room, linking the two spaces.

traditional fabrics as I wanted to put back a little bit of the history of the building. Then it was easy, and within two days I knew which fabric to use.' The couple added red accents to the scheme, spending four years looking for dining chairs in just the right shade of red, and Robin found a chest-of-drawers in Berlin with different coloured façades to finish off the space. 'It's been a labour of love to make it personal and a real family home,' Lisa says.

Above all else, their home reflects the couple's carefree attitude. Their design choices are stylish and show an innate sense of colour, but are also practical, such as the vinyl flooring, which their teenaged boys and their friends skateboard across, and the patterned sofa in the snug, which, despite its glamorous looks, is robust enough to withstand the wear and tear of family life.

Left and above An Art Deco lamp, a humorous 'Vanity Kills' sign, framed fashion prints and numerous art books reflect the couple's interests and tastes.

Opposite On the top floor is the luxurious master suite, complete with a bath in the bedroom.

'Our home is comfortable, inspiring, bright, fun
and not too precious,' Lisa says. 'It has different
personalities and feelings, and our things tell a story
about us as people. It's very real, and will never
feel like a hotel or a shop window. It's quirky, and
somewhere to relax and be yourself.'

Activist artist
Converted warehouse | Soho

Above On the walls are paintings either by friends, or given to Martin as gifts.

Opposite Martin brought a collection of garden urns from his previous home to remind him of happy times spent there. They are now on display in his sitting room.

Martin Firrell is known for his large-scale and dramatic works of public art, which have seen him described as both a cultural activist and a philosopher. He aims to stimulate positive change in society through his work, and to open up debates about issues such as liberty, diversity, justice and the human experience. Using film, the Internet and photography, most famously projecting thought-provoking messages onto the sides of buildings, including St Paul's Cathedral, Tate Britain and the Houses of Parliament, he hopes viewers will respond to his work by thinking about how to lead a happier and more fulfilled life. Martin finds his own fulfilment in his loft space in Soho, a somewhat quieter space than those he works with. 'I call my home the monastery, or the ark,' he says, 'and I try to create the feeling of a peaceful retreat here.'

Making full use of living in the heart of central London, Martin dines out daily but rarely entertains at home, preferring to keep his private space calm and tranquil. 'The things I choose to have at home are very calming, because a lot of my creativity comes from my anxieties,' he explains. 'I try to affect the texture of the moment, because the only thing we can be sure of is this actual moment in our lives.' This approach is played out in the way Martin has furnished and decorated his home, ensuring that he is surrounded by only those objects and furnishings that have real personal meaning. 'Most of the choices about what I have in my space are made

because they connect me to people,' he says. 'I don't think I have anything where I don't know the person who made it.' A portrait of Martin by his sister and drawings by his mother hang on the walls, while an antique arm-chair and gilt mirror that used to belong to his grandmother and now sit in the open-plan sitting room reflect Martin's French heritage. Mementos such as the framed pair of ballet shoes, which belonged to a friend who wore them during his last ballet performance, are on show, as is an orange chair in the bedroom, bought at a friend's charity auction. In the sitting room, urns that used to sit in the garden of Martin's Norfolk house are a reminder of a previous home. 'I never have any of my own work out, because I don't want to live with my own work when I can live with other people's,' he says.

Martin was lucky that his flat did not require any structural alterations when he first moved in, and the only addition he has made is a guest bathroom next to the living space. He knew he wanted to live in the flat as soon as he stepped through the door: 'I loved the seven windows, as seven is a heavenly number, and the floor felt like an incredible old wood-block floor in Paris, with its beautiful patination.' Martin kept the decor neutral, choosing earthy tones to keep him grounded. 'I went through a beige and brown phase, even though I don't really like brown, but it is a calm earth colour,' he explains. He sits in the same seat at the table every day to work, and finds that the views provide him with all the inspiration he needs. 'I can look out of the windows and see the sky. I quite like the way I can see all my favourite pictures from this position, and I put movies on my computer, which I can contemplate in the background while I edit my films. Language is very powerful, and I feel that works of art should help us lead better lives.'

Above Martin's BAFTA award and a pair of ballet shoes worn by a friend are among some of the treasured objects on display.

Above and left A painting of Martin by his sister hangs in the dining room, where he sits down every day to work, looking out over the Soho rooftops. The antique chair is a reminder of Martin's French heritage.

Following pages The floor- to-ceiling windows were the reason Martin bought the flat when he first saw it. His style is simple and personal, and includes many references to close friends and family.

Product designer & fashion stylist
Warehouse conversion | Victoria

Marc Newson & Charlotte Stockdale

As one of the world's most influential and accomplished designers, Australian-born Marc Newson has designed thousands of products, from trainers for Nike and restaurant interiors to a concept car for Ford and a jet plane – even a space ship. His 'Lockheed Lounge' chair holds the record for the highest price (over $2 million) ever paid for a piece of furniture. Married to Charlotte Stockdale, a stylist, contributing editor to *Vogue* and creative director for Fendi, the couple live in a converted Royal Mail sorting office in Victoria, near Westminster Cathedral, with their two young children. 'It's the nicest place I've ever lived,' says Marc, 'and it's fantastic for the kids.' This is a family home that pushes the boundaries of design to their limits.

Marc is well known for the flowing, organic lines of his designs, and the couple's home is no exception. A vast space (120,000 sq ft) with big windows and lofty ceilings, the flat is both a showcase for his designs and a spacious family home. The family had previously lived in Charlotte's more traditional London townhouse, but found that living over five floors was just not practical with small children. The open-plan layout of the flat is not only showstoppingly original, but is also much more practical for life with a young family. When Marc and Charlotte bought the apartment, it was just an empty brick shell. They put in an additional floor, allowing for a double-height ceiling in the sitting room and dining space, with the mezzanine-level guest bedroom acting as a bridge between the two sides of the flat. In the sitting room, an impressive wall of natural stone provides texture, and the

Below Artist Julia Lohmann's 'Cow Bench' sits in the sitting room. Against the opposite wall is Marc's 'Voronoi' shelf, carved from a single piece of marble.

Above The ground-floor space features a number of Marc's designs, from the 'Medium Lathed Table' and 'Diode' lamp in the corner, to the kitchen itself. The counter top is made from a single slab of marble.

Following pages The library at the heart of the home is a complete contrast to Marc's modern style, with bespoke wood panelling and a sofa covered in tweed from Colefax & Fowler.

wood floor and antler chandelier are a nod to luxury ski lodges. 'I've always liked those big chalet-style homes, like in the movie *North by Northwest*,' says Marc, 'and I wanted to re-create that feel here.'

Amazingly, Marc has no formal design training, having studied jewelry and sculpture at Sydney College of the Arts before moving to Tokyo, where he designed his first products. The couple are now based between London and Paris, and are away for more time than they are at home, so the comforts of home are particularly important to them. In the centre of their apartment, a traditional panelled library provides an unexpected contrast to the modern design throughout the rest of the flat. Walls of shelves display books, magazines and family photographs, and two comfortable sofas face each other in front of an open fire. This cosy space is Marc and Charlotte's favourite room, and is where the family spends most of its time.

Left and below The bedroom is decorated with wallpaper inspired by fractals, designed by Marc especially for this room. Charlotte's more traditional taste is seen in the antique chair, which sits in front of green storage units, also designed by Marc.

Opposite The bathroom is wall-to-wall marble, chosen for its pattern of continuous stripes.

'My experience as a designer is invaluable, because I'm confident about what will work,' Marc says. 'It was a great opportunity to do exactly what we wanted, as opposed to having to stick to a brief or wrestle with somebody else's taste, as I do in my day job.'

Kate Halfpenny & James-Lee Duffy

Stylist and designer &
art director and illustrator
Mews house | Camden

Above A Venetian chandelier hangs in the bedroom. In the hall, a collection of vintage prints and an antique metal trellis lend interest to the space.

Opposite Kate's wedding-dress designs are kept in the sitting room, which doubles as a studio for fittings.

The mews house in Camden belonging to Kate Halfpenny and her partner James-Lee Duffy is testament to their combined creativity and love of vintage furniture and design. This is the third mews house that the couple have renovated, transforming it into a quirky home that doubles as a work-space for them both. Kate, a bridal-wear designer and stylist who began her career by working for Vivienne Westwood before launching her own label, and James, an art director and graphic designer, have combined their antiques and collectibles with contemporary design to create a cosy and stylish live/work space.

Kate and James bought the house while living at the other end of the street in another mews house, which they had also renovated. Kate was looking for another project to get her teeth into, and wanted a home that could double as a studio, as well as somewhere comfortable for her celebrity clients to visit for consultations. The house ticked all the boxes, and clients such as models Kate Moss, Erin O'Connor and Daisy Lowe and actress Emilia Fox regularly visit the studio for fittings. James also works from home, so it was essential that the couple's new home provided enough space for both of them.

The house needed to be completely gutted and renovated when Kate and James moved in, so they set to work removing the cheap laminate floors and pine fittings, polishing the foundation concrete underneath and replacing the frosted-glass partitions by the front door with an antique metal trellis that Kate had shipped from Los Angeles. Kate created mood boards for the kitchen at the rear of the house, and installed crisp white units and antique-style tiles and fittings, with a range cooker at its heart. An open-plan dining and living space also doubles as a showroom for her bridal designs, and is filled with quirky furnishings, comfortable sofas and a large

dining table, over which hangs a striking chandelier in sunny yellow. Kate's studio is in an adjacent room, where she and her seamstresses painstakingly hand sew vintage lace and beading onto her exquisite designs.

On the top floor is James's studio, where he works for clients such as Nintendo and Coca Cola, as well as contributing to the cult art-zine he founded, *Pavement Licker*. His space is distinctly masculine, and reflects his love of popular culture and street art. Also upstairs, the master bedroom and en-suite bathroom provide a relaxing space for the couple to retreat to after the working day. Kate has decorated the whole of the house with her trademark flair, using strong, dark colours in the bedroom and bathrooms, with layered textiles on the beds and antique armoires providing much-needed storage.

Above The sideboard in the dining room is fashioned from an old shop cabinet, which still has its original lettering on the front.

Opposite Also in the dining room, a Venetian chandelier and vintage yellow chairs stand out against the blue-painted wall.

Left and below In James's study, graphic-art books share shelving space with his collection of toys.

Opposite The study has a more masculine feel than the rest of the house, with its industrial-style desk and chair, and pendant light overhead.

'I am uncensored in the way I choose pieces,' says Kate, 'and very instinctive and impulsive. The fabrics dictate to me how I design my dresses, and I design my interiors the same way, starting with a material or a piece that inspires me.'

Above and right Quirky objects and gifts from friends are dotted about the house, including an owl, poised in mid-flight, in the master bedroom.

Opposite The couple chose inky blue tones for their bedroom, mixing an antique mirror and chandelier with an oversized charm bracelet on the wall.

Priscilla Carluccio has a photographer's eye for detail and composition. Her riverside home, a modern flat designed by architect Richard Rogers, overlooking the Thames near Battersea Park, reflects her refined aesthetic and thoughtful approach to styling. Her belongings are organized and carefully arranged in groups, while her furniture is considered and understated, but still immensely stylish. The end result is a glamorous space that has the feel of a gallery or beautiful shop, but manages to be welcoming and homely at the same time. 'Because I was a photographer, I can select what I want very quickly, and that was fantastic training for the eye,' she says. 'My home is very light, with clutter about, but it's organized clutter.'

Priscilla is a respected authority on design, having been appointed Creative Director of the Conran Group by her older brother Sir Terence Conran (father of Sebastian Conran; pages 118–25), and later becoming Habitat's international stylist and Head of the Product Studio. She then joined Paola Navone to create Due Mani, developing handicrafts in the Far East, before co-founding the deli-café group Carluccio's with her then-husband, chef Antonio Carluccio. After leaving Carluccio's, Priscilla opened the eclectic, much-praised shop, Few and Far, on the Brompton Road, selling beautifully designed objects that appealed to her own aesthetic, including homeware, clothes, jewelry and old-fashioned roses.

Priscilla moved to the flat from a townhouse in Fulham, which she had shared with her children and grandchildren. 'The house was able to absorb

Below A selection of red cushions are piled up beneath vintage paintings, while a collection of suitcases that reflect the overall colour scheme are displayed in the sitting room.

Above The flat enjoys panoramic views across the Thames to Battersea Power Station.

Following pages A floor-to-ceiling shelving unit contains objects collected from around the world. In the study, the desk chair is a classic design from Tolix.

my kids and their kids, but they grew to a stage where they didn't need it and having a house became irrelevant,' she explains. 'I wanted to live in a more modern space, and when I saw this, it was obvious to me that it was the one.' It was the flat's light and airy interior and the natural flow of the space, together with design details from clever hidden storage to the finishes on the doors and windows, which appealed to her, and its simplicity provided a dramatic blank canvas for Priscilla's collections of curiosities and design, amassed over a lifetime. 'I wanted to surround myself with more contemporary furniture as a backdrop to all of my things,' she says. 'I've spent years collecting, and my trail through life has been very much about looking and selecting. I love hunting and gathering for my shop or for my home.'

Priscilla has not altered the design or layout of the apartment since she moved in. 'It's the only place I've lived in where I haven't felt the need to change anything,' she says. She brought her huge iron table from Conran with her, along with her Paola Navone sofa, while other pieces of furniture were acquired on buying trips for Few and Far. Family portraits sit alongside groups of collectibles, while a palette of red, white and silver keeps the overall look cohesive and polished. Priscilla spends a lot of time at home, and entertains regularly. 'I think people feel welcomed here, and are amazed by the river,' she says. 'They really seem to like the place.'

James Russell &
Hannah Plumb

Hannah Plumb and James Russell are JamesPlumb, two artists working together under one name. The couple met while studying fine art and sculpture at Wimbledon College of Art, and now create assemblages, and interiors from salvaged and forgotten pieces, combining a unique, time-worn beauty with a functional aesthetic. The pair love unearthing objects and redesigning them to give them new purpose and meaning, from 'Sampson', a light crafted from a broken toy with a lampshade as a head, to 'Anne and Jack', a collection of nine luminaires crafted from former shade-maker's stands. 'We feel like match-makers, matching objects to make something new,' explains Hannah, 'but they feel as though they could always have been together.'

Such has been their success since launching their studio in 2009 that they have been commissioned to design several high-profile interiors, and their collections have enjoyed international acclaim. Their home, a two-up, two-down Victorian cottage, once tied to a former Wesleyan chapel next door, has a Dickensian feel to it, and is sensitively decorated in sooty

Above The couple's cottage was once connected to the beautiful chapel at the bottom of the garden, just visible through the window.

Opposite The dining room is a cosy space with an antique table at the centre and a bench upholstered in French mattress ticking. The pendant light is one of the couple's own creations.

Opposite The couple found the kitchen units one by one, putting them together to create a quirky space with plenty of shelving. The colours used throughout the cottage were matched to specks of the original paint found at the back of cupboards.

Below The couple's first creation together: a luminaire called 'Sampson'. In the sitting room is an antique button-back armchair, which sits beneath vintage wallpaper and fabric pinned to the ceiling.

colours, and furnished with reclaimed objects, into which the couple have skilfully breathed new life. The cottage, which sits alongside two other tiny houses on a residential street in Stockwell, has an other-worldly feel to it, like stepping back in time to a forgotten past. Barely visible next to the neighbouring Victorian terraces, Georgian villas and impressive Regency-style chapel, the cottage's unassuming exterior gives few clues to the treasures that lie within.

Hannah and James have taken care to enhance the innate character and soul of the building, by carefully peeling back layers of plaster, tile and laminate flooring to reveal the bare bones of the structure. Throughout the ground floor, they replaced the flooring with reclaimed boards from the Royal Doulton factory, and pieced together a kitchen from antique cupboards found at auctions and antiques fairs, and a handsome 1950s fridge bought from a market in north London. Open shelves display delicate flower arrangements in tiny plant pots, bright-red tomatoes on the vine and a selection of vintage kitchenalia. Without space for a roll-top bath, the couple were forced to buy a more contemporary design, but disguised it with some lead and old tin ceiling panels, adding little bits of decorative detailing as they went along. Hannah and James have tried to reuse everything they could, and the design of the house evolved as ever-more layers were peeled away to reveal its historic past.

Right and below Tiles and plaster were removed in the bathroom to reveal the original brickwork. The beams were left exposed to gain additional ceiling height. In the bedroom, heavy canvas was fixed to the ceiling, inspired by antique campaign tents.

Opposite The headboard is made from antique cupboard doors from Josephine Ryan; the canopy above was part of a 1920s changing tent. Vintage suitcases have had their lids removed to create a clever and unusual chest of drawers.

'I remember having a meeting here with a buyer from Liberty, and she asked to use the bathroom. I panicked because there were horrible sea-horse tiles in there, so I took a hammer and chisel to them and these delicious bricks started appearing. We couldn't cover them up again, so we built the bathroom around them.'

Graham Judkins

Interior designer
Edwardian mansion-block flat | Maida Vale

Having lived in the hippest areas in London, from Notting Hill to London Fields, interior designer Graham Judkins and his partner Anne wanted somewhere quieter to bring up their young daughter Stella. Their search took them as far as Norfolk before they found their two-bedroom flat in an Edwardian mansion block in Maida Vale. Despite being 'an oasis of calm in a busy city', the flat needed extensive renovations, which Graham, who co-founded Untitled Design Studio with his friend Mick Birch, was happy to take on, as it gave him the opportunity to redesign the space to his own exacting standards.

'The flat was in a really bad state,' he recalls, 'which allowed us to re-configure it with the emphasis on living space.' He put in underfloor heating beneath a limed oak engineered floor, and knocked down several walls to create two bedrooms at one end, separated by a sliding wall, as well as a shower room, kitchen and living room. The couple were keen to introduce a contemporary feel, so Graham didn't replace the skirting boards and architraves, which had been removed by the previous owners,

Above 'Hang It All' hooks by Charles and Ray Eames, beneath a Banksy print, add colour to the hall. In the kitchen, the black-painted wall is a dramatic contrast to a pendant light by Muuto at Skandium. The chairs are also by Charles Eames, as is the table base; the table top was custom built by a friend.

Opposite An Eames rocker sits next to a sideboard by Arne Vodder, bought from Two Columbia Road. On top is a collection of Lyngby pottery.

'Our idea was to keep the bedroom small, because we just sleep in there,' says Graham. 'We wanted to open up the space and create somewhere you live, not just somewhere you exist.'

Opposite The couple chose a space-saving bed with storage, covering it with a bedspread from Melin Tregwynt. Above is Louis Poulsen's 'Artichoke' pendant light, which was allowed to rust in their Norfolk barn to give it an aged look. In Stella's bedroom, Graham designed the bed himself to create a den underneath. Another print by Banksy hangs in the bathroom.

Below Stickers from Supernice adorn the walls in Stella's bedroom. The family dog finds that a vintage chair topped by a cushion from Design House Stockholm is just the right spot for a snooze.

resulting in a clean, minimalist space. 'Designers and architects hate skirting boards and they'll spend a fortune avoiding them,' he explains. 'The whole flat needed to be taken apart and put back together again, so that is what we did.'

The flat now flows seamlessly, following the lines of the limed oak flooring. Graham designed the kitchen himself; the cabinet doors, made from plywood panels from Tintab and fitted to carcasses bought on the high street, were arranged to line up with the grouting of the tiled floor. 'Our builder is a wonderful craftsman, and built the whole place with extreme precision,' says Graham. 'The plywood is pretending to be solid wood. Because you can't really get wood that wide, we've taken a natural material and engineered it to find an honest solution to show that it is manmade and has its own beauty.'

Once the renovations were complete, the couple set about moving their impressive collection of mid-century modern furniture and graffiti art into their new home. Years of scouring design stores and obsessively bidding on furniture online has resulted in an enviable collection of design classics, including the Robin Day chairs in the sitting room, bought on eBay, and the Arne Vodder-designed sideboard, purchased from the couple's favourite shop, Two Columbia Road. The huge collection of graffiti art by the likes of Banksy, Eine and Paul Insect is a reminder of the couple's roots in the East London design scene. The flat's considered and thoughtful design, created with the family's needs in mind, has resulted in a stunning space for Graham and Anne to enjoy and for Stella to grow up in.

Claire Durbridge & Bob Sakoui

Fashion stylist & art director

Edwardian converted flat | Brondesbury

Above Animals cut out from wrapping paper have been used to decorate the nursery. Next door, the conservatory walls are covered in a striking stripy design.

Opposite Claire chose 'Pompeian' wallpaper by Cole & Son for the kitchen, and painted the table legs turquoise.

As a successful fashion stylist and art director, Claire Durbridge and Bob Sakoui know a thing or two about personal style. The couple first fell in love with their two-bedroom flat, an Edwardian conversion in the north-west neighbourhood of Brondesbury, because of its wide entrance hall and lofty ceilings. Rather than being put off by its need for a complete style overhaul, Claire and Bob saw this as the ideal opportunity to put their individual stamp on their new home.

Describing the flat as 'colourful, eclectic and a bit bonkers in parts', Claire has largely been responsible for the quirkily eccentric decor, which has developed organically since the couple first moved in. 'We haven't tried to achieve any particular look or feel,' she says, 'but have simply bought and chosen things that we love.' She is the first to admit that she can sometimes go a little bit over the top when it comes to embellishments, adding ribbons and tassels where perhaps others wouldn't, but it is her enthusiasm and talent that have brought a unique creative vision to the family home she and Bob share with their two young children.

The biggest structural change the couple made to the flat was to connect the kitchen to the living room, creating an open-plan living and dining space, linked by an archway. The kitchen, with its distinctive geometric wallpaper, is a relaxed family room with freestanding units and vintage furniture, including dining chairs from the 1950s, while in the sitting room, the original fireplace, cornice and architrave lend a somewhat grander feel, with a comfortable sofa and retro leather chair and coffee table adding a dash of vintage glamour. Objects and collectibles, such as a sculpture of the Eiffel Tower, line the mantelpiece and provide plenty of talking points for visiting friends.

In the master bedroom, botanical prints that have been torn from an art book and framed hang on the wall, while a bespoke headboard with integrated shelving and lights is a sleek yet practical design. Claire's creativity has really been let loose in the extraordinary conservatory, which doubles as a formal dining space and playroom, where black-and-white striped wallpaper gives an Alice-in-Wonderland feel. The adjacent nursery is decorated in Liberty prints and sophisticated shades of grey, creating a playful but stylish room for the children to grow up in.

The unusual decorative scheme continues in the entrance hall, where the back of the front door has been painstakingly painted by Bob in a graphic geometric design; reclaimed cinema seats and a series of mirrors in various sizes and shapes add to the theatricality of the space. The uniting factor among all the creative details in this quirky home is a passion for colour and pattern, and a talent for combining the two. 'Bob and I have different tastes,' says Claire, 'but between his design ethos and my busy, eclectic style, we match very well.'

Opposite An otherwise ordinary entrance hall is turned into a dramatic space by painting the back of the front door and adding a row of old cinema seats.

Below In the master bedroom, an antique French armchair sits beneath a series of framed prints taken from an art book.

Following pages A bespoke headboard features recessed shelving and built-in wall lights; the bathroom is decorated in 'Lily' wallpaper by Cole & Son and an antique mirror.

Artists
Converted pianola factory | Kentish Town

Laura Ford and Andrew Sabin's search for a home where they could both live and work led them to a deserted cash-and-carry warehouse, formerly a pianola factory, in a conservation area in Kentish Town. The couple, who met at Chelsea College of Art and are now two of the UK's leading sculptors, with work in collections around the world, needed a space that could both contain their studio and provide a home for them and their growing family, and the warehouse seemed the ideal solution given their very specific needs. 'The amount of light and space it had made us fall in love with it,' says Laura. 'And it had great access for getting sculptures in and out.'

The Victorian building was completely derelict when they found it in an auction catalogue, but despite its broken windows, leaking roof and cracks in the walls, the couple saw its potential and bought it for the equivalent price of a one-bedroom flat. Used to creating large-scale works of art, they were undeterred by the amount of work that needed to be done, and did as much of it as they could themselves. 'As sculptors, we have a lot of practical and visual skills,' explains Laura. 'It's not everyone who has a forklift

Above A light-filled courtyard is at the centre of the family home. Sliding glass doors allow light to flood into the huge studio on the ground floor.

Below One of Laura's fabric sculptures – part human, part animal – shown in progress in the couple's studio.

Following pages The couple designed and built the shelves and desk themselves, using their well-honed practical skills.

and an arc welder.' They demolished partition walls, removed ugly security grilles and managed to patch up the roof. 'Holes had been cut through the floors, so that boxes could be dropped through,' recalls Laura. 'It was a bit chilly in the winter, but it was good fun and the kids could roller skate around the living room and not worry about messing it up.' Working with Clerkenwell-based Kennedy O'Callaghan Architects, the couple came up with a design that was economically viable without losing the character of the building, and formed a company with their builders to deliver the project. Andrew made the steel structure, the three staircases and the kitchen, and helped out on most of the build, ensuring that they got exactly what they wanted and that costs were kept to a minimum.

When it came to decorating and furnishing their new home, Laura and Andrew were equally hands-on and imaginative. 'Andrew has used a lot of steel in his work in the past, and I use a lot of fabric, so we pooled our skills to make all the main pieces of furniture ourselves,' Laura says.' We love our huge 10ft-long sofa, which all the family can sit on.' Having done so many exhibitions, the couple are adept at setting things out within a space, ensuring that they look their best, but remain practical and low-maintenance: 'On a trip to India, we stayed in a hotel that basically got hosed down every day. That inspired us, because although our place is not quite like that, practicality has always been a priority.'

Left One wall in the master bedroom is covered in a classic wallpaper design by Fornasetti for Cole & Son.

Opposite A vintage dressmaker's dummy is home to a collection of handbags, cameras and other accoutrements of family life.

Collection
Wed. nigth
* RECYCLING
* Compose
* NICO'S SCHEDULE *
- MONDAY
SWIMMING = 3:30 – 4:00
- WEDNESDAY
GYMNASTIC – 4:00 – 5:00
- THURSDAY
BALLET – 4:00 – 4:40
Nico has playdate with

Jo Berryman

Interior designer
Victorian house | Hampstead

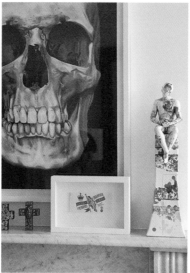

In the leafy neighbourhood of Hampstead, designer Jo Berryman has channelled her passion for interiors, fashion and music to create the ultimate rock-chick pad. Describing her style as 'British eclectic with a dash of Hollywood Babylon', her talent for creating unusual juxtapositions – such as pairing an industrial concrete floor with a French gilt sofa – make her the interior designer of choice for anyone wanting a sophisticated interior with a bit of bite. Jo bought her three-bedroom Victorian house on the edge of Hampstead Heath following her divorce from Coldplay bassist Guy Berryman, and added a simple conservatory and mezzanine at the rear. She also created the ultimate indulgence – the whole of the first floor as her own master suite – where she can relax in her roll-top bath each night. 'My bedroom inspires my work,' she says. 'I often come up with interior solutions in an alpha state of half-sleep.' A separate dressing room houses her huge collection of vintage and designer clothes, many acquired when Jo worked as a fashion stylist and owned a boutique.

On the lower ground floor, the open-plan kitchen and dining room provide a comfortable family space for Jo and her daughter Nico to relax in, complete with a large draper's table surrounded by Hans Wegner chairs. Two walls covered in blackboard paint allow Jo to note down reminders about Nico's schedule for the week ahead, and a floor-to-ceiling shelving unit in oxidized steel completes the space: 'I love it because it allows me to display chaos in an orderly fashion,' she says. On the floor above is a formal sitting room, where guests can relax on a vintage modular sofa found in Alfie's Antique Market. Jo wanted the space to be evolving and functional, as well as a place to display her growing collection of art and curiosities, which adorn the walls and mantelpieces. In the adjacent room, with a view to the mezzanine and the kitchen below, a large table by Eero Saarinen

Above Found objects sit side by side with treasured artworks, such as this blue and white figurine by Pierre Williams, bought at the Affordable Art Fair.

Opposite An antique Louis-style sofa, found at the Ardingly Antiques Fair and re-covered in velvet, shares a corner of the kitchen with a large framed photograph and a cactus plant.

Above and left In the kitchen, a collection of vintage and modern crockery, cookbooks and other bits and pieces are displayed in an industrial-style shelving unit. The dining table is an old draper's table, originally from Rose Uniacke's studio.

Below A red stair runner is a dramatic foil against the white-painted floorboards and walls.

Below The cosy seating area next to the kitchen boasts a deep-buttoned chesterfield sofa and a starburst mirror, found at Alfie's Antique Market.

Following pages In the first-floor sitting room is a vintage curved sofa from the 1970s. Above the white-lacquer sideboard is a wallhanging by Vivienne Westwood for The Rug Company. The 'Bristol' sign is from an antiques shop in Fulham.

is overlooked by Damien Hirst's *Memento Mori* skull and Peter Saville's *Unknown Pleasures*. Jo uses this room for meeting clients and exploring ideas, explaining that she finds the light conducive to brainstorming.

A glamorous hallway, painted in pale grey with a dramatic red stair runner and chandelier by Gino Sarfatti, leads to the upper floors, past the master suite, up to a guest bedroom and Nico's bedroom at the top of the house. Believing that a home should reflect its owner's life experiences, Jo's own house is a glamorous and carefree mix of music, fashion, art and design. 'I live, work and sing wholeheartedly within every nook and cranny, I'm a karaoke nutcase,' she laughs.

'I tend to use grey tones for connecting spaces like landings and halls, and colour in bedrooms or to define pockets of detail,' Jo says. 'I experiment a bit more boldly with ideas at home than I do with clients.'

Above The headboard in the master bedroom was designed by Jo, flanked by 1950s Italian bedside tables from Circus in Kensal Rise and Art Deco lamps from Cristobal.

Opposite The master suite, complete with dressing room and roll-top bath, occupies the entire first floor. On the floor is a design by Giles Deacon for The Rug Company.

Opposite Sebastian's 'Radius' tables sit in front of shelves on which books are arranged by colour – a habit he says he inherited from his father.

Below Sebastian was attracted to the house because the front door is at street level, making it easy to get his bikes in and out.

As part of the Conran dynasty, the name that has been at the forefront of British design for over fifty years, it is not surprising that the home of the acclaimed product designer Sebastian Conran is a supremely stylish space. Sebastian, son of Sir Terence Conran, and brother of fashion designer Jasper and homeware designer Sophie (as well as nephew of design entrepreneur Priscilla; pages 72–77), lives with his wife Gertrude in a semi-detached Victorian terraced house in Bayswater, which he likens to New York City because of its buzzy, creative atmosphere. His home is his retreat, and is where he spends most of his time: 'Home is where I feel safe and like to be as much as possible, apart from my studio,' he says. 'I always have projects on, and there is always something to do or fix. I don't get country cottages and spending hours travelling to and fro. In fact, I really do not like travelling at all.'

Sebastian found the house in 2002, and felt as though serendipity had led him to it. 'When I was a child my step-aunt lived in the house next door, and I always thought I would like to live in a house like that,' he recalls. He also loved the fact that the ground floor is at street level, rather than up or down a half-flight of stairs, which is good for bicycles (of which he is a fan), and the potential to create a huge open-plan space. 'The garden was dead, the place was infested with mice, there was a rather shoddy extension and no fenestration on the windows,' he recalls. 'It felt a bit soulless and unloved.' But seeing the possibilities in turning it into a warm and functional home again,

Sebastian ripped out the whole of the ground floor, stripping the walls back to the bare brickwork and the floors right down to the earth, before putting in a new floor, walls and ceilings. The result is a series of rooms that function both separately and as one interconnected space.

Although Sebastian does have his own work around the house, including the 'Radius' table, which he designed for Universal Expert, and his range of homeware for John Lewis, he prefers to live with furniture, art or objects that he has been given or collected along the way – things that tell the story of his life. One wall in the living area is covered entirely with framed punk posters from Sebastian's student days (while studying at Central St Martin's School of Art, he famously got the Sex Pistols their first booking). He attributes his modernist, eclectic taste to his father – an influence that can be seen in the way he arranges his books. 'Having grown up in my father's house, been a roadie for The Clash, interested in mechanics and passionate about making and inventing things, they all show their scars,' Sebastian says. 'I have a lot of bits and pieces, so I wanted an airy, neutral space with lots of light so that it didn't get cluttered.'

Opposite Folding glass doors slide open to join the dining room with the garden.

Below A collection of paintings amassed over the years hangs in the sitting room.

Following pages Beautifully crafted furniture is skilfully combined with antiques and artworks to create a unique and personal home. The kitchen is a cool combination of wood and stainless steel.

Neisha Crosland

Textile designer
Victorian terraced house | Clapham

Above In the courtyard garden at the centre of the house, Neisha planted such evergreen plants as jasmine and kiwi.

Opposite Artist Ian Harper created the 'Japanese Tree' mural in the dining room; gold and copper leaf add to its luminous quality.

Having trained at the Royal College of Art, and honoured with the title Royal Designer to Industry in 2006, Neisha Crosland is now one of the UK's foremost textile designers. She launched her first collection in 1994, and has since designed rugs, wallpaper, tiles, bed linen, stationery and a range of homeware and fashion accessories that are much loved by designers and stylists around the world. She lives with her husband in a converted mews house near busy Clapham Junction, which they discovered in 1992 when looking for a home that could also offer the space to build a studio. The house was the only building in the row to survive the Second World War, and was surrounded by wasteland, which meant that, unusually, they were able to rebuild and extend it. 'It looked like a postage stamp on the back of a postcard, set in the flattened, bombed-out land,' Neisha recalls. 'I loved the mix of decrepit 1940s architecture and the fact that it was enclosed by lovely brick walls and cobblestones, which made it feel secluded.'

The couple rebuilt and restored the building bit by bit over a twenty-year period, extending it to meet their needs, but keeping the original cobblestones, doors and dark-green window frames. One of the first things they did was the landscaping, creating a secluded garden where they planted star jasmine, kiwi vines, trees and lawns. Because the planting is evergreen, visitors can imagine that they are in a garden in Tuscany or Provence, rather than in a little corner of south London. The house is now L-shaped and looks onto a courtyard garden with a small fountain; the mature gardens give the feel of a rural escape. 'I love the idea of living in the city, but feeling like you are in the countryside,' says Neisha. 'The Romans twigged that it was boring in the country, so they decorated their city homes with interior gardens with running water and trompe-l'oeil paintings of landscapes, which is what we've tried to create.'

When it came to decorating, Neisha was in her element, cheerfully making mistakes and persevering until she got it right. 'I had a box full of photographs, tear sheets from magazines and photocopies from books as inspiration. It was the same process as designing my own work,' she says. 'I started with a chaotic wealth of ideas, which were very confusing, and then edited out what I didn't want. I contemplated everything, painting huge samples of paint à la Rothko on the walls, pinning swatches to chairs and living with it all, and even then I made mistakes, repainting the sitting room three times before I was happy! My thing was just to make it cosy and comfortable.' By introducing luxurious textiles, warm materials and plenty of colour and pattern, this is exactly what she has achieved.

Below Neisha's sister, interior designer Charlotte Crosland, designed the bespoke stainless-steel kitchen. The patterned tiles are from Danish company Made a Mano.

Opposite An intricate hand-painted mural, patterned tiles and unusual light fittings add personality to Neisha's home.

Following pages Dining chairs from Christopher Howe are each covered in a different colour from Neisha's 'Plains' collection.

Above and left The doors in the master bedroom were designed by Neisha and made by Jim Howett at Marianna Kennedy. The handles were originally from a palace in India.

Opposite In the master bedroom, Neisha designed the chairs herself and covered them in her own 'Diamond' fabric. The headboard is upholstered in fabric from Leonie Brown.

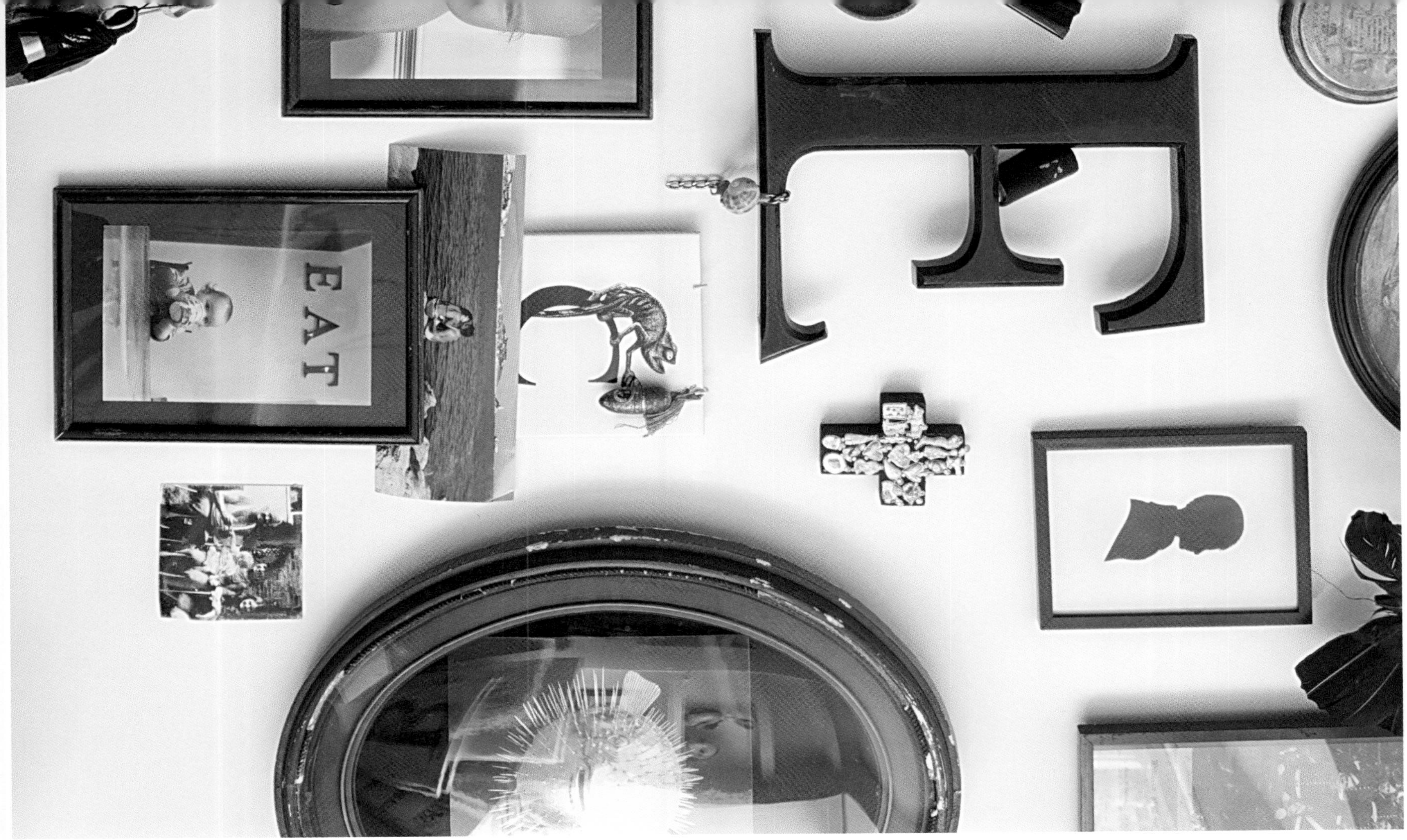

Rory Dobner

Artist
Victorian maisonette | Hampstead

Artist Rory Dobner and his wife Claire have lived all over the world, from India to Hong Kong, Australia to Taiwan, but the north London village of Hampstead is where they call home. They first became enchanted by a small two-bedroom flat in a handsome Grade II-listed mansion block in 2003. Set back from the road and overlooking a 'magically secret garden', the building was so hidden away in the warren of alleyways and back streets that the estate agent had almost given up on finding it. But the couple persevered, and were won over by the flat's exposed beams, flag-stone flooring and original woodwork, none of which had been altered since 1850, when the building was first completed. Finding out that Sid Vicious and Johnny Rotten of the Sex Pistols had once squatted in the building sealed the deal.

Since buying the flat, which did not even have a kitchen or bathroom when they moved in, Rory and Claire have completed an impressive amount of structural work. First on the list was digging out the basement to create a kitchen and dining room, along with a glamorous black-tiled family bathroom, involving digging through yet more layers of thick clay soil, avoiding the underground river, and carrying it out by hand to the nearest road through the neighbouring gardens and winding side streets. The couple then bought the flat next door, undertaking a lateral conversion to create a further bedroom and family bathroom on the ground floor, so that their two young sons, Louis and Huxley, could have their own rooms.

Opposite In the sitting room, an elegant button-back armchair has been re-upholstered in purple satin. The rug is by Vivienne Westwood for The Rug Company.

Below Downstairs in the kitchen, a grey velvet sofa from George Smith provides a cosy seating area. Up above in the hall, the original flagstone floors remain. The back of the front door has been covered with blackboard paint for the children to write on.

Above A stag's head and a painting by Rory in black gloss on brushed stainless steel add interest to the stairwell. The tiles are also Rory's own design.

Opposite The bedroom is a calm and serene space, with a muted colour scheme and luxurious textiles.

Following pages In the light-filled studio next to the kitchen a bespoke black wooden desk provides plenty of work space. Above, custom-built storage keeps unwanted clutter at bay.

Lastly, they bought the land behind and next to the property, extending into the garden to create a double-height studio space for Rory, next to the kitchen. The result is a warren of rooms that the family jokingly calls 'Hampsterville'.

Claire, an energetic force of nature, had worked all over the world for British Telecom, while Rory was a stay-at-home father until a buyer at Liberty saw one of his wildly imaginative and eccentric drawings. Since then, his drawings and wire sculptures have become so popular that he can barely keep up with demand. Rory frames all of his work himself (using antiques he has collected) in his light-filled studio, where he works at a 5m-long bespoke desk. Together, the couple have worked hard to respect the homely character of the flat that they first fell in love with.

'We've thoroughly enjoyed ourselves, experimenting with building our own bespoke kitchen from school tables, playing with colour and trawling salvage yards for reclaimed bricks, flooring and fittings,' Rory says. His own work pops up all over the flat, while many of the objects, including playful pieces of taxidermy like 'Albert' the duck, or vintage collectibles displayed on the window sills, mantelpieces and walls, are recognizable from his pictures. 'We love the unusual, items with character that talk to you, that have a past, and we can't resist naming lots of them, because characters have to have names.'

'Our home is slightly bonkers, just like us,'
Rory says. 'We're a bit like magpies, so we
really try to self-censor so as to not overindulge.
But it's a rule that has failed miserably.'

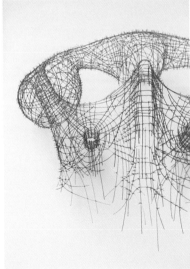

Above and left Known for his eccentric drawings of animals, Rory keeps plenty of little creatures around the house for inspiration.

Opposite A toy rabbit sits on the windowsill, surveying the view, while elsewhere beetles adorn a wastepaper bin. Rory's designs are also featured on the sofa cushions.

Textile designer
Victorian terraced house | Willesden

Textile designer Margo Selby still lives in the family home in Willesden, north-west London, that she grew up in. These days, she shares the three-bedroom Victorian terraced house with her daughter Cleo, and has decorated each room in her trademark palette of vibrant colours. 'I have to try out designs at home, because I need to know what it's like to live with my designs,' Margo says. 'It helps me to understand what works and doesn't work, and what I want to do next. I've realized that I love living with yellow and green and that I like light spaces.'

When Margo's father first moved into the house with his young family, it was decorated with wood-chip wallpaper and gas fires hung precariously from the walls. He updated the property, adding an industrial kitchen from which he ran a successful catering and event business. Now that Margo shares the house with Cleo, she has softened the kitchen by painting it in bright colours, and altering it to suit her more modest cooking needs. It remains at the heart of her home, next to the sitting room and leading to a pretty courtyard garden. Margo has laid new wood floors throughout the house, and painted the few walls that she has not covered in her own bold designs. The house has a welcoming feel, enveloping friends and family in rich colours and patterns, luxurious fabrics and personal touches.

In the sitting room, wallpaper, a sofa and rugs, all of Margo's own design, together create a warm and comfortable living space, with the elegant furniture offset by her collection of art and ceramics. Designer friends often

Below The industrial-style kitchen was brightened up by painting it blue and adding such homely touches as a painting by a close friend. Behind, wallpaper designed by Margo can just be seen.

Above A pair of boots made from handwoven fabric sit on top of a rug in the sitting room. In the bedroom more of her designs, from the wallpaper to the bed linen, sit alongside family heirlooms.

Following pages The stair runner was designed especially for the house. Margo's innate sense of colour and pattern is clear to see throughout her home.

give Margo examples of their own work at craft and design fairs (swapping them for items from her collections), which now have pride of place in Margo's home, complementing the handmade quality of her own work. A sofa, the first piece of furniture that she designed, takes centre stage, while her luxurious textiles are found everywhere, from the cushions in the sitting room to the runner on the stairs and the colourful bedspread in the master bedroom.

Margo's work has a beautiful handwoven quality, cleverly combining surprising colour combinations to create stunning three-dimensional designs, and reflects her background as a weaver and artist. She trained at Chelsea College of Art and Design, the Royal College of Art and later at the Ann Sutton Foundation, a centre for research into woven textiles, and launched her first collection in 2003. 'I'm influenced by the emphasis on making art, and my work evolves on the hand-loom, where you have to learn to mix the colours with your eye,' she explains. 'I've always loved bright colour combinations, repetition and order, and I've done a lot of travelling and been inspired by craftspeople.'

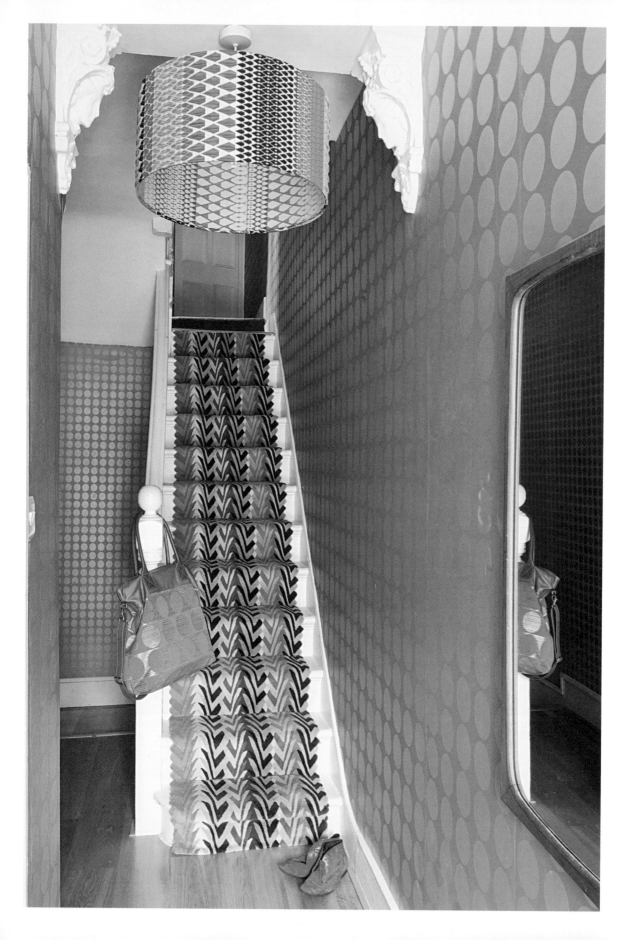

Joelle Talmasse & Martyn Gayle

Interior designers
Ex-council house | Notting Hill

When Joelle Talmasse and her husband Martyn Gayle, who together run the interior design and bespoke furnishings company Breaad, first viewed their ex-local authority house in Notting Hill, they planned to buy it as a rental investment. But once they got inside and saw the potential of the space, the couple decided to make it their next family home. Taking inspiration from the large loft apartments they had previously lived in, Joelle and Martyn set about completely remodelling the house, removing walls to open up the first floor into a large open-plan kitchen and sitting room, and create two bedrooms for their daughters on the second floor with a master bedroom in the attic. Cutting-edge technology was added, along with a bespoke kitchen, new bathrooms and flooring made from reclaimed wood, to create a home that was both economical and eco-friendly.

When it came to the interiors, the couple found that the house was the ideal blank canvas on which to project their vision of truly bespoke living and sleeping spaces for their young family. Joelle originally trained as an artist and painter, but after working for the likes of designer David Champion, from whom she learned the art of technical drawing, she turned to interior design. She tries to evoke the feeling of a space in her work, creating montages of photographs, drawings and fabric samples to communicate her ideas, and has designed the interior of her own home with her unique creative flair. Martyn, who was previously a successful hairdresser, working on shoots for *Vogue*, *I-D* and *The Face* magazines, collaborates

Below The couple are keen collectors of modern design classics, including the twin chairs and floor lamp at the foot of the stairs.

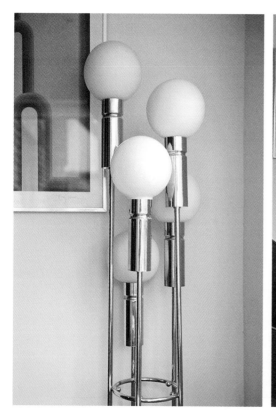

Above A denim-clad bench and lamp, both designed by Joelle and Martin, bring a humorous touch to the sitting room. The use of black creates a dramatic look for the kitchen.

with his wife to design and produce furniture and lighting collections, examples of which can be found in their home. 'When we met we had all these great ideas together, so we decided to start collaborating,' he says. 'I made several prototypes for lighting and furniture, which we showed at Maison et Objet in Paris, and the response was amazing. We were asked to go and exhibit in New York and Milan, and it took off from there.'

In the sitting room, the couple used bold colours and combined their own designs with customized vintage furniture. The couple's work can be seen throughout the house, from the cushions adorning a large, French-inspired sofa to a theatrical bench covered in vintage denim and rhinestones, and overlooked by a lamp customized with more denim. Vintage dining chairs were repainted in bright pink and turquoise to complement a Pop-Art print on the wall, and artworks by many of the couple's friends feature throughout. Black has been used to dramatic effect in the kitchen, bathroom and bedrooms, making the bold colours stand out even more and giving the house an edgy, contemporary feel. For the girls' bedrooms, Joelle created playful yet grown-up rooms, filled with quirky touches from cushions covered in vintage denim to customized chandeliers.

'We wanted to create a unique space,' Martyn says. 'We're very eclectic and rock 'n' roll in our taste, and it's certainly not minimalist. We like to put our own spin on things and put our personalities into our work.'

Right and below A steep, custom-made staircase leads up to the master bedroom on the top floor. Warmth has been brought into the space by leaving the exposed bricks untouched and adding artworks and cosy textiles.

Opposite Vintage bookshelves, running along a floor made from Pirelli rubber, now provide storage for the couple's shoes and hats.

'We wanted something with space in Notting Hill, which can be expensive and difficult to find,' says Martyn. 'At first we thought the house would just be an investment, but once we went inside, we realized we wanted to live there.'

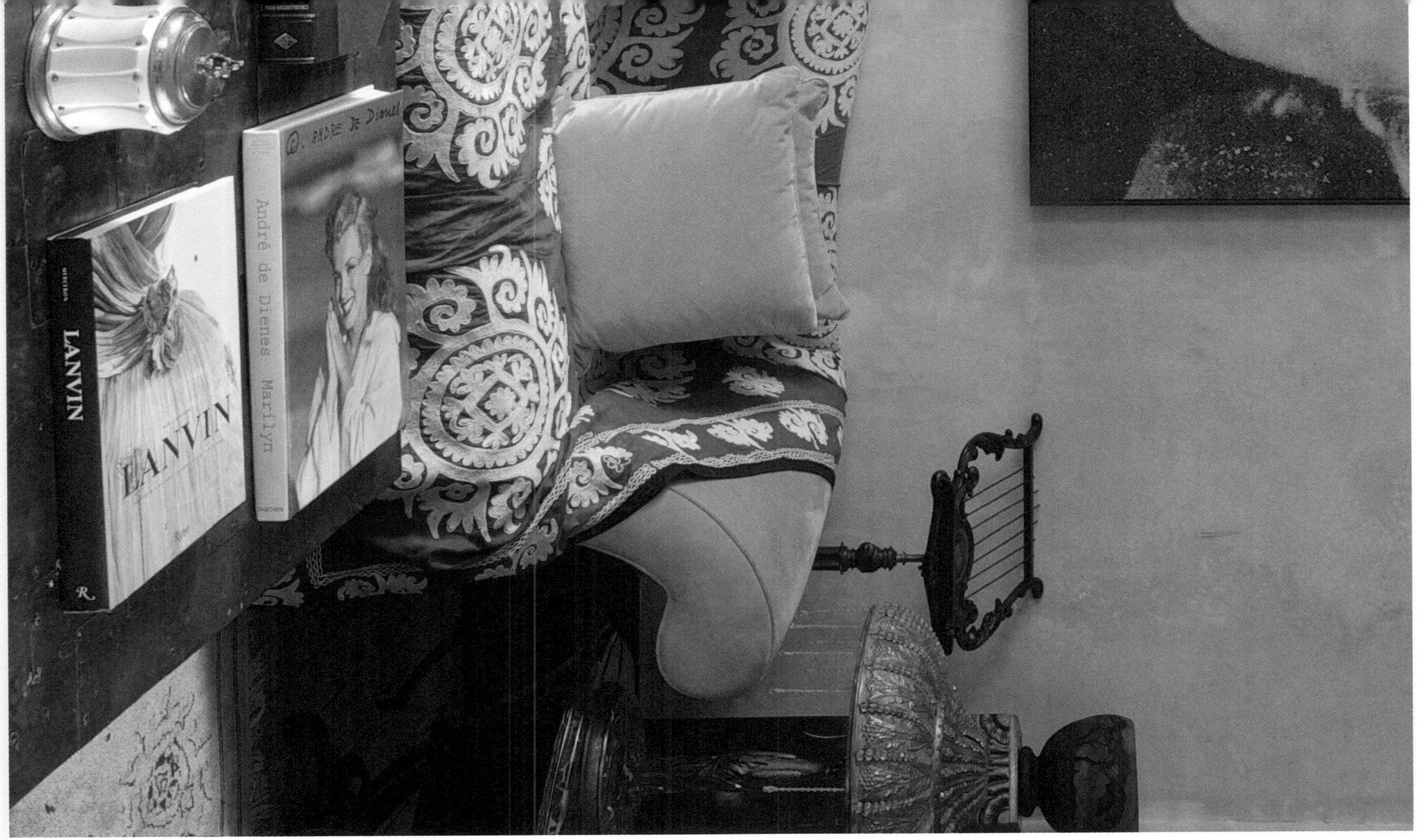

Jo Wood

Interior designer
Regency townhouse | Regent's Park

Interior designer Jo Wood had only looked at one other property before finding her four-bedroom, white-stucco Regency townhouse near Regent's Park. Having lived in London, New York and Los Angeles with her ex-husband Ronnie Wood, and toured the world with the Rolling Stones, Jo came full circle when she found her new home in an area she had lived in when she first came to London in the 1970s. 'As I walked up the steps to the front door, I knew this was it,' she says. 'It felt like coming home.'

Jo grew up in a creative household, and interior design came naturally to her. Her father was an architectural model-maker, her mother collected doll's houses, and her brother is the artist Paul Karslake. 'I remember my father making beautiful little houses with tiny rooms, and when I was nine and we moved into an old vicarage, my mother's life was all about doing it up,' she recalls. Years later, as soon as she saw this house, Jo knew what her vision for the interiors would be. 'I wanted plaster walls, bare floorboards, lace at the windows and lots of black,' she says. 'It was a blank canvas, and I wanted to make it look like I had been here a long time, not as though it had been newly decorated.'

Guided by her passion for vintage, Jo often buys furniture and accessories at the Paris flea markets, and the result is what she calls 'a cross between rock 'n' roll and Marie Antoinette.' It is a glamorous, bohemian home, dotted about with family photographs and filled with colour and

Above For the kitchen, Jo chose a range cooker and freestanding units to create a cosy space for entertaining. In the sitting room, a plush purple sofa adds warmth and colour.

Opposite Jo loved the texture of the bare plaster walls in the first-floor sitting room and decided to leave them as they were, adding French antiques to create a romantic look.

pattern. Jo project-managed the renovations herself, making sure she was on site every day to oversee each detail. She started by stripping back each room so that only the original details remained, and then had the whole house re-plastered. All of the wiring was replaced, and reproduction radiators were installed to give a period look, yet still be energy-efficient. The lower ground floor took up most of the renovations, as the space was originally a warren of tiny rooms. Jo created an open-plan arrangement, installing a new kitchen with vintage units and a range cooker. Her four children and six grandchildren gather together around the large farmhouse table in the dining space, which opens out onto the garden, or in the cosy snug next door.

'As I go along, I scribble little notes and drawings of how I imagine it to be and then go and look for things in auctions, reclamation yards and antiques markets,' Jo says. She bought one original fireplace with her from the home she shared with Ronnie in Richmond, in west London, and had a few pieces of furniture re-upholstered, but everything else from the house went to auction. She relished the opportunity to start anew, and, amazingly, the entire project was completed within just a few months. Jo has since been approached to design the interiors of several houses and a well-known nightclub, along with a range of accessories inspired by the experience of renovating her own home.

Above In the master bedroom, a series of framed prints hang above the French-style bed. Opposite the bed is a comfortable chair covered in blue velvet.

Opposite Jo created a glamorous space for her antique dressing table, also in the bedroom, complete with vintage chandelier and a tasselled stool.

Right and below The dressing room has plenty of space for Jo's vintage and designer clothes and shoes, collected over a lifetime. In the hallway, the black-painted stairs add a rock 'n' roll vibe.

Opposite The romantic, freestanding bath is one of the only pieces in the house that is not a genuine antique. Distressed furniture and framed portraits all lend to the feeling of faded grandeur.

'I'm mad about interiors,' Jo says. 'I didn't find anything a struggle when doing up the house, because I loved doing it so much. It was all I ever thought about, and now I just love being here.'

Jewelry designer
Modern flat | Notting Hill

Having decorated her two-bedroom contemporary flat in Notting Hill in a kaleidoscope of jewel-bright colours, Pippa Small now describes being in her home as 'like floating on the inside of a rainbow.' She divides her time between designing jewelry collections for the likes of Tom Ford at Gucci, Phoebe Philo at Chloé and Nicole Fahri, and pursuing a lifelong interest in anthropology. Pippa has worked with the San people of the Kalahari desert in southern Africa and the Kuna in Panama, helping them develop their traditional designs as an aid to self-sufficiency, and her home is a reflection of her passion for the colours used in the crafts of indigenous cultures – a constant source of inspiration.

Pippa first fell in love with the flat because of its sense of space, and she immediately set about introducing colour to the white walls and functional, bachelor pad-style kitchen. Working with her good friend, the painter Gail Arnold, she removed the black cupboard doors and repainted them a bright turquoise, installed a new wooden counter top and painted the walls in countless coats of natural lime. 'It was a joy to sit and dream up colours,' she recalls. 'We looked through books on plants and Indian miniature paintings, and at my collection of old textiles to find colours that inspired.' A carpenter made a bespoke shelving unit to house Pippa's collection of toys, as well as a chest of drawers for her precious stones.

When it came to decorating the open-plan sitting room, Pippa had no preconceived idea of what she wanted. Having collected furniture, artwork and textiles from around the world, she found that the brightly coloured walls provided a glorious backdrop to her Indian paintings, as did the cerise sofa for her collection of cushions from Uzbekistan, India and Bolivia. Pippa covered the floors in Turkish and Tibetan carpets, and added a cabinet that had been in her family for four generations. 'I realized

Above Dotted about Pippa's home are ceramics and curiosities picked up on her travels around the globe.

Opposite Brightly patterned textiles from India, Africa and South America adorn every surface in the sitting room. Striped rugs cover the coffee table, as well as the floor, set off by an eclectic collection of cushions and throws.

Opposite The master bedroom is decorated in a tranquil shade of aqua blue, with touches of pink. In the corner, a French chair has been given a modern revamp with vibrant fabric.

Below In the guest bedroom, books are crammed into every available inch of the bright-pink bookshelves.

I simply love colour,' she says. 'I can gaze at a tone of pink, or become enthralled by laying a lime-green fabric next to a canary-yellow cushion. Colour inspires me, and makes me very happy.'

On the other side of the sitting room, a large farmhouse table provides a workspace for Pippa during the day and a comfortable spot for entertaining by night. 'I can quickly sweep everything away into a cupboard and have the table set for twelve for dinner,' she says. It is overlooked by a vibrant painting by her sister, the artist Alex Small, who used pigments brought back from the Holi festival in India (see pages 166–67). Colour is also a key feature in the master bedroom, which Pippa painted a calming blue to remind her of her late mother. 'She died just before I moved,' Pippa says, 'and somehow the bedroom, with its long, elegant silk curtains and aqua walls, are a tribute to her.'

Above and right Pippa often takes her inspiration from the colours and shapes found in nature, as seen in this handmade peacock-shaped pendant, and keeps her collections of precious stones, shells and other objects in baskets and custom-built drawers.

Opposite Bright turquoise and lavender have replaced the black colour scheme of the formerly masculine kitchen.

East

Opposite Many of East London's warehouses, including this one in Shoreditch, have been transformed into desirable residences.

Following pages Adding to the more usual London housing stock of Victorian terraces are other types of dwelling spaces, such as houseboats and new apartment blocks.

Pages 178–79 One of the many historic terraces in Spitalfields. Once derelict or used as sweat shops, these houses now change hands for vast sums.

Creatives from all walks of life have long been drawn to London's East End, attracted by the affordable rents, energy and cultural diversity. This hipper half of the city has undergone a transformation in recent years, from gritty, often derelict, urbanscape to desirable (and expensive) residential neighbourhoods. Areas such as Shoreditch, Stepney Green, Dalston and, south of the river, Bermondsey, offer a thriving artistic scene in the heart of East London's centuries-old industrial fabric. From the Huguenot immigrants who settled in Spitalfields in the seventeenth century to the explosion of the Bangladeshi community around Brick Lane in the 1970s, to the film producers, fashion designers, artists and entrepreneurs who inhabit the East End today, each has left their own mark. The legacy of generations of Jewish, West Indian, Turkish and Vietnamese settlers is apparent in the variety of cuisines found throughout the area, and the tolerant attitudes of its residents have made it a magnet for artists and artisans. Today it is possible to wander from Hoxton's designer boutiques to Spitalfields market, taking in art galleries, picking up a bagel in Brick Lane, and ending with a meal at a Michelin-starred restaurant in the formerly notorious Bethnal Green. In the area around London Fields, a new café, antiques shop or microbrewery seems to appear in one of its abandoned railway arches every week, while a saunter along the canal takes walkers to London's docks in one direction and Islington's Georgian townhouses in another. Edgy, cool and vibrant, the East End is never short of surprises.

Architect Chris Dyson has been a key figure in the regeneration of the historic neighbourhood of Spitalfields, which has since become one of the city's most fashionable locations. Until Chris came along in 1991, the neighbourhood's beautiful eighteenth-century houses, many of which had been home to the Huguenot immigrants who settled in Spitalfields and established a thriving silkweaving industry there, had been neglected for decades and used as sweat shops or accommodation for restaurant workers in nearby Brick Lane. Since then, Chris has restored numerous houses in the area, and counts the artist Tracey Emin and writer Jeanette Winterson (who owns the fruit and veg shop Verde in Brushfield Street) among his many clients. 'I found that I loved it,' he says of his move to the area. 'I couldn't imagine being anywhere else.'

The house that Chris, his wife Sarah, a modern languages teacher, and their two children Oliver and Bella live in is a clever blend of period style and contemporary design. The restoration involved a dramatic rebuilding of the entire front elevation – although onlookers today would never guess that they were not looking at the original façade – and extensive renovations to the interior. Chris spent hours studying the *Survey of London*, a multi-volume historical and architectural survey of the city, published by English Heritage, and designed the front of the house to the specifications of Sam Worrell, the original architect in 1720, so that it sits harmoniously with its neighbours. The project took ten years to complete, and involved a period of living in yet another Huguenot house, now the office for Chris's architectural practice.

At the top of the building, Chris created an open-plan master bedroom, bathroom and dressing room for himself and Sarah, complete with a roll-top bath and a cupboard that was hand-painted by an artist friend. A chest

Above The view from the master bedroom takes in the spire of Christ Church Spitalfields, designed by Nicholas Hawksmoor and completed in 1729, and the iconic 'Gherkin' beyond.

Opposite When Chris bought the house there was only one niche in the ground-floor reception room, so he had an exact copy made for the other side of the fireplace. The painting above the mantelpiece is by a friend.

Opposite In the first-floor hall, which looks through to the sitting room, Chris added eighteenth-century pillars and a door surround from Lassco. The flooring is from Solid Floor.

Below The panelling in the sitting room and the downstairs dining room was designed to be in keeping with the house's eighteenth-century origins.

from Solid Floor (see Eelke Jan Bles; p. 242) sits in front of the simple four-poster bed. The drawing room on the first floor is a comfortable space, in which period elements such as wood panelling, polished floorboards and chandeliers sit alongside modern furniture designs by Matthew Hilton. The room is kept devoid of clutter, with books and television hidden cleverly concealed by panelling or within the chimney breast. In the ground-floor reception room, two alcoves sit on either side of the central fireplace – one original to the period, sourced from architectural salvage firm Lassco, and the other a modern re-creation, painstakingly copied by Chris's carpenter.

The extraordinary thing about Chris's work is that each building he renovates feels as though it has always been that way, such is his sensitivity to period style and attention to detail. His own kitchen, however, is unashamedly modern, while the garden, designed by landscape architect Luis Buitrago, boasts a metal walkway and huge New Zealand ferns. It is this harmonious juxtaposition of old and new that makes this restoration so successful.

Above and left The addition of modern elements enhance the historic bones of the house. On the wall is *The Map of Spitalfields Life*, by Adam Dant.

Opposite Treasured objects and gifts from friends are displayed in the older of the pair of niches in the ground-floor sitting room.

Following pages In the master suite, a copper roll-top bath from William Holland adds a touch of modern luxe.

'I've had a bit of fun, because the house isn't listed. A friend led me to buy things from the 1720s, the period when it was built, which we've included and copied to complete the look. You have to follow the details through so that it looks right.'

Above The kitchen and dining room on the lower ground floor have a fresh, modern feel, thanks to furniture designs by Matthew Hilton and high-gloss white paint on the ceiling to maximize the light.

Opposite Wood cladding and a metal walkway were added to the rear elevation and garden. The front façade is a faithful representation of how the house would have originally appeared.

Sarah Fry

Costume designer
Converted jam factory | Bermondsey

Costume designer Sarah Fry has created her own interpretation of New York's famous loft spaces in her own flat in a former jam factory in Bermondsey, a south London neighbourhood historically associated with the city's tanning trade and now home to a bustling antiques market, as well as such cultural institutions as the Fashion and Textiles Museum (see Zandra Rhodes; p. 232), skilfully combining modern design with vintage furnishings to create a home that reflects her personality and lifestyle. 'I had a file of images of Manhattan lofts and I love quirky collectibles, so I wanted a space where they would sit comfortably within the bones of the space I had inherited,' she says. Sarah, who has been television and radio presenter Jonathan Ross's personal stylist for several years, bought the flat soon after she started working in television. She designed the huge open-plan kitchen and living space, two bedrooms with en-suite bathrooms and an office herself, only employing a builder to make her vision a reality.

The industrial staircase was the sole feature in the flat when Sarah bought it, and reflected the type of interior she hoped to create. 'I loved the existing features of the concrete floor, exposed brick walls and the fantastic riveted columns, so when I introduced other materials they were either complementary or sympathetic to the mood,' she says. She sourced industrial light fittings and reclaimed oak strip flooring from a school gym, which she offset with a high-gloss kitchen and simple monochrome walls

Above Sarah painted the floorboards in the entrance hall black, with floral wallpaper and floating storage adding to the dramatic look. The bedroom and bathroom are on the lower level; the steel staircase leads up to the living area above.

Below In the kitchen, units from Ikea were customized and installed by Sarah's builder.

Following pages An illuminated sign, made by Sarah's partner Richard for the set of a television show, has pride of place in the living space, alongside a vintage Louis-style armchair and a retro leather sofa.

to achieve the loft-style look that she wanted. The build took ten months, with Sarah doing much of the work herself at weekends. She wanted the space to feel cosy, despite its lofty proportions, and so she used lots of large pieces of furniture, artworks and quirky pieces from work or travels to bring the flat to life. Painting the kitchen black helped to keep it from feeling cavernous and sterile.

Sarah visited interiors showrooms in New York's Soho to find inspiration for the kitchen, and asked her builder to create a Carrie Bradshaw-style walk-in wardrobe for all the clothes she collected through her work as a stylist. Sarah, who now shares the flat with her partner Richard Drew, a production designer, describes her style as 'definitely eclectic', and furnished her home with finds from antiques shops, vintage fairs and car-boot sales. 'My best bargain is the Minnie Mouse bedside lamp, which cost a pound at a jumble sale,' she says. Her talent for styling is reflected in the decoration: 'I have a fixation with styling things and telling stories, creating characters and putting things together,' she says. 'I'm planning to stay here for a while because the area has changed so much since I bought the flat, and now we can pop out for great coffee or an amazing meal. I just wish I could finish it!'

'I fell in love with the flat because the building had such a handsome exterior and it was a huge empty shell,' Sarah says, 'which meant I could build my dream space from scratch.'

Above and right Sarah added a roll-top bath and pretty accessories to create a feminine en-suite bathroom. A huge portrait of Barbara Streisand, a prop from the Jonathan Ross show, hangs in the bedroom.

Opposite An alcove behind is a handy space for a shelf. Quirky vintage finds add to the fun and flirty feel of the room.

Michael Smythe

Artistic producer
Victorian warehouse studio | Shoreditch

Photographer, artist and producer Michael Smythe was so determined to make his home in this block of Victorian artists' studios in Shoreditch that he walked past it every day for two years, waiting for a space to become available. When a studio finally became vacant, he asked all his friends to bombard the estate agent with low offers so that when Michael eventually looked around it and made his own offer, the agent was so relieved to have found someone who was serious about taking it on that he offered Michael the space straight away.

A founding member of Nomad, an art and exhibition collective, Michael has produced several exhibitions and installations at the Old Vic Tunnels in London, as well as producing his own films and three-dimensional works. He had been living abroad before returning to London in 2002,

Above Pots and pans hang from hooks on the walls of the narrow galley kitchen. An industrial light from Rochester's hangs overhead. The shower room is beyond.

Opposite The building has always been artisan studios, with plenty of exposed brick and original features.

'I need as much space as possible to think clearly, and I don't like clutter or decoration,' Michael says. 'I don't need a lot of stuff. I grew up with parents who are hoarders, and I think it's a reaction to that.'

Above Examples from Michael's collection of globes and taxidermy are displayed on shelves above his desk.

Opposite Other vintage treasures include framed butterflies and a stack of antique suitcases.

Following pages The view from the studio into the open-living space, where Michael works and sleeps.

and promised himself that he would find a home with the largest possible windows to compensate for the poor natural light, reasoning that if his plants could grow well in a space then he could, too. 'It is a very communal way of life here,' Michael says of the building, 'with lots of people coming and going, bringing what they do into the building, which, being a durable, practical space, facilitates that.'

Michael's studio had previously been the office of architect David Adjaye, who installed the heating and additional lighting. Keen to respect the building's 120-year history as a working studio, Michael left the original floorboards exposed, so that the hundreds of nails hammered into them by the craftsmen of yesteryear remain as a reminder of its former life. He prefers a minimalist aesthetic, and his few clothes are stored in a small drawer beneath shelves bursting with books, magazines and a collection of globes, one of the few objects he collects. 'I only collect globes and taxidermy because I find them very nostalgic,' he explains. 'The globes remind me of that feeling of potential as a child, and I'm drawn to taxidermy because I grew up on a farm. I find the Victorian pieces very beautiful.'

The studio is on the upper floor of the two-storey building, and still has the original windows, beams and full-height warehouse-style doors. The exposed brick walls and stripped floors contribute to the period feel, but can also make the space feel cold in the winter months, so a wood-burning stove was installed. A farmhouse table, found in an antiques market in France, provides Michael with a comfortable space to work at, as well as to entertain friends for dinner. An industrial lamp from his close friend Mark Rochester, a dealer in vintage furniture and lighting, hangs overhead. 'I keep prints and things that are either sentimental or relics from projects,' Michael says, 'but I'm pretty ruthless and I don't hold on to much.'

Mawi Keivom

Jewelry designer
Victorian villa | Dalston

Opposite The table in the entrance hall was originally bought as a desk for Mawi's shop; the screen above was a vintage find.

Below Because of its corner location, the house is wider than its neighbours. The staircase is original, and the floorboards have been left bare.

Born in northeast India and raised around the world, jewelry designer Mawi Keivom worked for fashion designers Isaac Mizrahi and Bill Amberg before launching her own eponymous label in 2002. Her eclectic take on heraldic symbols, combined with period influences and contemporary design, quickly saw her pieces being worn by the likes of Kate Moss, Alexa Chung, Elizabeth Jagger and Daisy Lowe, while she herself became a favourite with international fashion editors. Mawi and her husband and business partner Tim, himself the son of an antiques dealer, have created a unique home, filled with items collected on their travels around the globe.

When the couple first saw the sprawling Victorian villa in Dalston, dubbed 'the coolest place in the world' by *Vogue Italia*, it was in need of extensive renovations, but luckily the original cornicing, fireplaces, sash windows and other features were still intact. The move into their new home was typically unconventional. 'Because we had to move between London and Milan fashion weeks, we moved in with the previous owner, with all his stuff still here, waiting for him to move out,' remembers Tim. The remodelling of the house is a work in progress, with much of the original paintwork and wallpaper continuing to be revealed. The house stands proudly on the corner of a long terrace, its position giving it a substantially more generous footprint than its neighbours, with a large, sweeping entrance hall and grand staircase. The lower ground floor is home to a kitchen/dining room with a long farmhouse table, covered in an antique lace tablecloth and surrounded by mismatched chairs. The couple's collection of vintage china and soda siphons are housed in a glass-fronted cabinet, on standby for unexpected guests who might pop round for impromptu cocktails.

Above, on the ground floor, the sitting room has been opened up from two separate rooms into one large space with a formal seating area at one end and an antique desk overlooking the garden at the other. Victorian

Above Mawi's beagle finds a sunny spot atop a comfortable sofa in the sitting room.

Opposite Downstairs in the kitchen and dining room, mismatched chairs and an antique dining table give the open-plan space a homely feel.

chesterfields sit alongside Art Deco side tables, ethnic textiles and Indian artwork, with Persian rugs covering the polished floorboards. At the top of the house, Mawi has the luxury of two dedicated dressing rooms, home to a fraction of her vast collection of vintage clothes and accessories, stored in cabinets that had previously displayed designer Linda Farrow's sunglasses collection for Liberty. The master bedroom is a bright space, painted in warm ochre and featuring a headboard covered in a blue silk kimono. Mirrored bedside tables and lamps add glamour, with vintage textiles providing comfort and warmth. Each room has been decorated with an eclectic mix of furnishings and textiles that reflect the couple's love of period details and diverse cultures.

'When we go and look at things for our home, nothing is based on price,' says Mawi. 'It has to be something you love, whether it's expensive or not. It's about what fits into our lifestyle, and we love whatever makes our home cosy and nice to live in, rather than considered or stylized.'

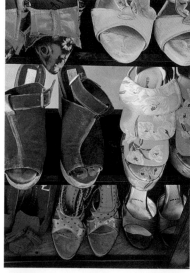

Above and right Mawi's collection of textiles and accessories is kept in former shop-display cabinets in her dressing room.

Opposite In the master bedroom, a headboard covered in a kimono and an Art Deco-style bedside table add glamour. The brightly patterned antique rug ties the colours together.

David Carter

Interior designer
Georgian terraced house | Stepney Green

Interior designer David Carter has enjoyed international acclaim for his eclectic and witty sense of style. Despite having no formal training in design, he found fame when his former flat in Islington was featured on the front cover of *World of Interiors*, and the founding editor, Min Hogg, contacted him with the promise to feature any future projects. David, who had been working in fashion but always had a passion for antiques and interior design, did indeed go on to fill more than forty pages of the magazine with his designs for clients around the world. 'The people who approach me want something different,' he says, 'something quirky and completely bespoke. If you've worked hard for your money, then you deserve to have the house you want. Live out your fantasies and have fun!'

His elegant early Georgian townhouse in Stepney Green is replete with architectural details, from eighteenth-century panelling to wooden-box cornicing, and has no fewer than eight original fireplaces. David has furnished his house with a highly individual mix of modern and antique furniture and art, from seventeenth-century chairs to contemporary works of sculpture by Mark Brazier-Jones, and added theatrical flourishes to every room, with giant pom-poms, masks, whips and top hats now adorning every surface. 'I love referencing all sorts of different periods and trying to capture the spirit of an age,' he says. 'It's more about playful historical references, rather than pedantic historicism.'

Above The sitting room is decorated in dark hues and luxurious textiles, inspired by the spirit of the 1920s and the decade's fascination with the Far East.

Opposite In the entrance hall, a statue of Christ on the cross is unconventionally attired in a top hat and slippers.

Opposite At the other end
of the ground-floor sitting room,
the Oriental-inspired theme
carries through to the carvings
of the windows and coffee table,
floor cushions of red silk and
a chinoiserie wall panel.

Below David created a paint effect
on the ceiling of the first-floor
music room, reminiscent of the
sky. The giant pom-poms are a
fun alternative to the more usual
chandelier.

The building was built in 1717 by John Ireland, part of a row of houses, originally named Ireland's Row, which forms one of the earliest uniform terraces left in London. David bought the house from the Spitalfields Historic Buildings Trust, and was awarded a substantial grant from English Heritage towards the restoration. 'The grant was awarded on the condition that we respected the fabric of the building, and restored as much as we could, using what was left as a template,' he says. 'In the sitting rooms, the wooden-box cornicing turned out to be a huge job to re-create.'

When David started work on the house, it had no roof and was derelict, inhabited only by pigeons. It took two years of major structural work to make it watertight and habitable, before any serious restoration or decoration could begin. David used what remained of the original panelling and cornicing on the first floor to replicate the original features throughout the house, and painted many of the rooms himself, creating a different story in each room. 'A good home is like an autobiography,' he says, 'and should reflect your life, your tastes and your passions.' This love of storytelling fuelled much of the design: on the ground floor, he created a sensual drawing room inspired by the brothels and opium dens of Shanghai, frequented by wealthy travellers in the 1920s, while his bedroom is an homage to Marie Antoinette's boudoir at Versailles. 'I love mixing styles,' David says. 'It's all about composition, colour and textures.'

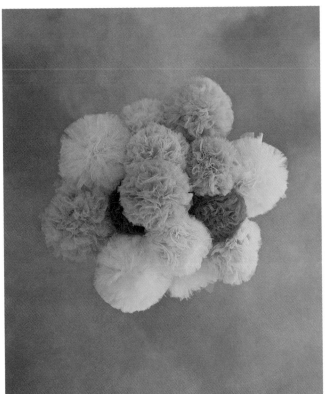

Above and right Many of the items in David's collection were given to him by artists he regularly commissions.

Opposite The house is full of humorous details, from the statue of a dog in the sitting room to the faux fruit in a bowl in the kitchen.

Following pages A French day bed is the focal point in the romantic bedroom; above hangs an antique corona from Rosemary Conquest Antiques.

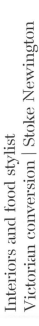

Alex Lewis

Interiors and food stylist
Victorian conversion | Stoke Newington

Having grown up in the Welsh countryside, interiors and food stylist Alex Lewis wanted to create a cosy, comfortable home inspired by nature's colours and textures when he bought his two-bedroom flat in hipster Stoke Newington. Alex, who has done work for brands such as Toast, as well as styling food for cookery books and commercial shoots, was won over by the flat's penthouse bedroom and panoramic views across north London from the roof terrace. As soon as he moved in, he set about designing an eclectic space in which to live and work.

Alex used the entire top floor as a painting and photography studio when he first moved into the flat in 2003, but soon found that he preferred the space as a bedroom because of the light and the views. 'The light is so wonderful, and you really feel the weather, rain or shine, when you look out onto the terrace and see big sky,' he says. 'That's what I was used to in Pembrokeshire, so it makes me feel relaxed.' Alex introduced carpet to the bedroom – a difficult decision given the beautiful reclaimed wooden floors that were already there – which makes it much cosier on cold winter mornings, and hung blackout blinds from the windows. He built a wall of storage with his own hands to run along one wall, and created a desk space and wardrobe, adding bookshelves above the bed.

In the open-plan kitchen and living room downstairs, Alex only needed to paint the kitchen units, adding shelving for all his kitchenalia. He

Below Family photographs, collected artworks and childhood memories are on display in the sitting room.

Above Alex's top-floor bedroom has doors that open onto a roof terrace. He keeps his collection of hats, shoes and props on display, or stored in vintage suitcases.

designed low-level storage in the sitting room to hide his television and hi-fi equipment, and kept the walls neutral to help show off his large collections of props, curiosities and memorabilia. 'Making my flat a cosy home was my only real goal,' he explains. 'I wanted a quiet retreat where I could be surrounded by things I have gathered along the way, and styling food books and interiors for a living means that I have a lot of props to find space for.'

Alex painted the hallway in green gloss paint, which reflects the light despite its dark hue: 'It's the first thing people comment on when they step through the door,' he says. Throughout his home, he tried to create a warm, comfortable and relaxed feeling, preferring to display treasured possessions, rather than expensive designer pieces. 'Being a country boy has helped me appreciate the beauty of objects,' he says. 'Simple curves and natural colours really appeal to me, and help with my styling choices. Just finding a moss-covered stick on a walk and bringing it back into my flat makes me happier than going out and buying some over-designed, over-priced homeware. I just want my space to feel homely.'

Left and below Treasured letters and photographs are kept in vintage albums. Paints, tape and scissors are a stylist's best tools. The green entrance hall has a welcoming feel.

Opposite The kitchen only needed a lick of paint when Alex moved in. He has since added an industrial-style pendant light and storage to the space.

Zandra Rhodes

Fashion designer
Penthouse flat | Bermondsey

Above A roof terrace with views across to London's newest landmark, the Shard, stretches around the perimeter of the penthouse flat.

Opposite In the living space, a golden 'Z' from Zandra's Bond Street shop shares space with a painting by Andrew Stahl and a mannequin named Ethel.

Legendary fashion designer Zandra Rhodes has had an extraordinary career, spanning more than forty years. Her bold designs have made her a fashion icon, and she has dressed everyone from Bianca Jagger and Debbie Harry to Diana, Princess of Wales and Kylie Minogue. With her trademark pink hair, blue eye shadow and theatrical outfits, her home is every bit as vibrant as she is. Zandra had always dreamed of creating a fashion museum in London, and in 1995 her dream came closer to being a reality when her friend, the artist Andrew Logan, spotted that an enormous warehouse building in Bermondsey was for sale.

'I looked at this giant building with a bomb site on the other side of the road, and realized I could bring all my work here and live in part of it,' Zandra says. 'So I moved everything into one building.' She sold her Notting Hill home, studio and factory to buy the warehouse, and persuaded architect Ricardo Legorreta to design it, painting the outside in her trademark bright-pink and orange. They built nine apartments to fund the conversion of the building into the Fashion and Textiles Museum, and designed a penthouse apartment for Zandra to live and work in.

In the open-plan living room, floor-to-ceiling windows provide panoramic views over Tower Bridge, Canary Wharf and the nearby Shard. Zandra had the entire room painted in the colours of the rainbow when she first moved in, and commissioned the tile company Antico to create the

swirling coloured floor to her specifications. Several artworks by Andrew Logan are on display, including mosaic busts of Zandra herself, colourful lamps and an enormous mirrored sculpture of Gandhi. Paintings by Dougie Fields and ceramics by Kate Malone and Carol McNicol are on display, along with chairs in the shape of the letter 'Z', created for Zandra's flagship stores in the 1970s. A mannequin named Ethel, resplendent in Zandra's own designs, oversees proceedings.

Zandra entertains whenever she is in London, often cooking for between ten and fifty guests, who sit round two circular dining tables. When she is not entertaining, the tables are used to display collections of treasured objects and her collection of rocks and crystals, many of which were given to her by friends. On the floor below, the pink bedroom is decorated with

Above Drawings from Zandra's latest collection in her studio downstairs. She keeps every screen from her entire career in the printing room below.

Above Below the flat, a small photographic studio documents a lifetime of work.

Following pages Zandra's rainbow-coloured living space on the top floor of the building. She outlined the colours in chalk when she first moved in, later adding works by Andrew Logan. The chairs were designed by Zandra for Expo 2000 in Hanover.

stencilled roses, which Zandra screenprinted onto the walls. Next to the bedroom is the library, with floor-to-ceiling bookshelves and photographs, lamps and curiosities that reflect Zandra's eclectic taste and interests.

Below is the hive of activity that is the office, studio and work rooms, with pattern-cutters and assistants busily preparing Zandra's latest collections. A labyrinth of rooms leads to the printing room downstairs, in the bowels of the building, where the patterned fabrics that she is famous for are still hand-printed. 'I've always enjoyed trying out different ideas and turning them into clothes,' she says. Her bright designs are still influencing the way we dress today. 'I think there is quite a lot now that is secretly influenced by what I do,' she says, 'but people don't even realize.'

Right and below Zandra decorated the lower floor of the flat in shades of pink and red. A library leads to the bedroom, where giant cabbage roses cover the walls and a pink chandelier hangs overhead. A gift from Andrew Logan hangs above the bedhead.

Opposite Art and design books fill shelves lining the walls of Zandra's library, and compete for space along with pictures and photographs, silk scarves and VIP invitations.

Eelke Jan Bles

Furniture designer
Industrial conversion | Spitalfields

For designer Eelke Jan Bles, Solid Floor, the flooring company that he founded in 1994, was only ever meant to be a supporting venture to finance his studies. It soon became a runaway success, however, with two London locations, and Eelke and business partner Robert Weems now also own the lifestyle and interiors shop Solid ID in Fulham. Having trained as both a photographer and architect, Eelke designed and built much of his home in the historic Spitalfields neighbourhood himself. Naturally enough, given that he founded a flooring company, wood features heavily in every room of the house.

Eelke bought the space in 1999 while working for a property developer. It had previously been used as a sweat shop, and was, as he describes it, a 'concrete box without windows'. Because of his previous experience of

Above Eelke drew on his vast knowledge of art, architecture and natural materials to create a welcoming, eclectic home.

Opposite Echoing his father's skills as a metal-worker, Eelke designed the walnut-and-steel kitchen table himself.

Above When Eelke first bought the building, there were no windows at the front and those at the rear had been blocked. Folding glass doors at the front now open onto a private courtyard, set back from the street.

Opposite In the living space, a row of phrenology heads and a bird skeleton in a glass jar are displayed above the desk.

warehouse living in nearby Shoreditch, Eelke wanted to retain the industrial feel of the building, injecting warmth and comfort through a liberal use of wood in the form of bespoke sideboards, lamps and cupboards, all made in his workshop. 'If you have a creative background and are in business, you don't get to produce anything real anymore,' Eelke explains, 'but I like to have a tangible thing at the end of a day.'

One of the first structural changes made was the installation of floor-to-ceiling glass doors, linking the interior to the cobbled courtyard outside. Adding windows to the rear of the building revealed views of Christ Church Spitalfields, and brought in much-needed light. Having found that he sleeps better in a smaller space, rather than one large, open-plan one, Eelke divided the house into a central living room and kitchen, with two bedrooms on one side and a wet room on the other. Keen to have the kitchen at the heart of the home, it is this space that first greets visitors as they step through the huge front doors. Eelke designed sleek panelled units, made from bamboo and wenge, along with the walnut and brushed-steel dining table, which sits at the centre of the room. Above it hangs a classic lighting design by Verner Panton. The floor, a mix of panga-panga and merbau wood, unites the kitchen and living space.

The only woodwork in the house that Eelke cannot lay claim to are the white storage cupboards lining the minimalist corridor, which lead to the wet room. Here, he was able to experiment with his love of unusual textures, choosing to plaster the room in concrete, despite the cracks. Of his wet room, Eelke says, 'I'm tall so I hate to be restricted, which is why it works, and the concrete and its textures are lovely with the ceramic sink. Everything I do is about texture.'

Above and right Minimalist
storage units run the length of
the corridor behind the kitchen,
leading to a concrete wet room
with a butler's sink.

Opposite Eelke originally planned
to live in one open-plan space, but
found that he prefers sleeping in
a smaller bedroom.

Ros Fairman

Artist
Victorian villa | London Fields

Above Ros uses the open-plan kitchen and dining space to create fantastical cakes with hand-painted fruit and flowers.

Opposite The marble floor in the kitchen formerly formed the floor of a Mappin & Webb store. The cabinets were made when Ros first moved into the house; the antique wooden island and stools were later added.

Artist Ros Fairman's home is a captivating blend of French rustic style and English eccentricity. Her talent for creating lovely vignettes from found objects and vintage curiosities means that every room in the four-storey, three-bedroom Victorian villa in London Fields that she shares with her husband Bob tells a story. The beautifully proportioned house, with huge sash windows overlooking the park, is painted in various shades of white to provide a backdrop for the antiques that Ros has collected over the past twenty-five years. She takes a painterly approach to decorating, building up layers of colour and texture by combining glittering light fixtures with crumbling plaster busts, portraits and plush furnishings. Mismatched chairs sit around a farmhouse table in the kitchen; elsewhere religious icons are mixed with bunting and gilt mirrors.

Ros bought the house in the late 1980s, and was attracted to it because of its size. 'I fell in love with the scale and the grandeur of it,' she recalls. When she bought the house, it had its original fireplaces, sash windows, cornices and ceiling roses, along with the original floorboards, revealed

when the carpets were removed. One of the few structural changes made was to open up the two reception rooms on the raised ground floor. Now one large space with sash windows at either end, it is filled with antique French sofas and chairs, giving the room the feel of a Paris salon. 'Often if you knock through two rooms, you end up with one end that no one uses,' says Ros. 'But having sofas at both ends makes it much more cosy.' The first floor houses a family bathroom and the master bedroom, and on the top floor, the couple knocked two bedrooms through to create a guest suite.

Downstairs, on the lower ground floor, Ros had the country-style kitchen fitted when she first moved into the house. She uses a freestanding island as a breakfast bar and preparation area, where she makes and decorates bespoke cakes for private clients, conjuring up creations fit for

Above A buttoned sofa in yellow silk provides glamorous seating in the sitting room, while a vintage drum makes an alternative side table.

Above The enormous French gilt mirror was Ros's first purchase when she bought the house, and sets the tone for the rest of the decoration.

Following pages The master bedroom is filled with vintage curiosities, including a sequinned costume and a statue of the Madonna. In the hall, a pile of antique suitcases provide stylish storage.

an eighteenth-century banquet, and hand-painting marzipan flowers and fruit to look as though they have tumbled out of an Old Master still life. A collection of glass cloches, china plates and objets d'art sit atop a wooden sideboard that takes up the length of one wall, while a traditional larder hides the fridge and provides additional storage. A retro jukebox is on standby for impromptu celebrations. 'The style of the house was never a conscious decision, it just grew from what I found,' Ros explains. 'I suppose you could call it a *folie de grandeur*.'

Jack du Rose

Jewelry designer
Warehouse conversion | Hoxton

When jeweller Jack du Rose received a real human skull by special delivery with a request to find out how to recreate it in platinum and diamonds, he had no idea that the artist who sent it was Damien Hirst, and that the skull was to become the controversial artwork *For the Love of God*, which would go on to sell for a record £50 million. At the time, Jack was only twenty-four years old and living with his parents in Birmingham. Now he lives with his fiancée in a stylish warehouse conversion near Hoxton, and has his own jewelry collection, 'Danger', launched at artist Sam Taylor-Wood's studio in Clerkenwell. Each piece of jewelry is crafted from precious stones and shaped in the form of a dangerous creature, in an ebony box and locked with a scorpion key made from diamonds, presented in a beautiful bell jar. This is an artist who pays keen attention to detail.

Above In the sitting room, Jack displays curiosities from around the world, including masks from Nepal and dolls from Laos. The sofas were found on eBay and the Chinese cupboard in a London saleroom.

Above Jack used tape to mark out the stripy pattern on the floor of his studio. The furniture, anatomy charts and chemistry bottles were sourced from antiques dealer Mark Rochester.

Heavily influenced by the work of the French glass designer René Lalique, Jack's fascination with the craftsmanship and artistry of the past is reflected both in his work and in his choice of furnishings for his home. Of his work he says, 'I wanted to create a brand that echoes how it used to be – to only make the absolute best, so that in years to come there will be a book with everything I've ever done, and each page will contain something as interesting as the next.' At home, he sourced furniture from auction houses and antiques fairs, and has a particular fascination with scientific paraphernalia, from a dentist's chair to a collection of physician's tools. For the open-plan sitting room, with its double-height ceiling, Jack sourced chesterfield sofas and industrial lights, and mixed it all up with a Chinese lacquered cabinet and examples of street art by London artists.

Display cabinets contain his collections of live snakes and insects, which serve as both pets and artist's models. (Jack's fiancée is a vet, and shares his passion for wild creatures, both dead and alive.) Artworks and interesting objects from their travels adorn the walls, and a large wooden dining table and chairs provides plenty of space to accommodate friends who drop round for dinner. In the studio, furniture sourced by vintage specialist Mark Rochester provides both inspiration and an evocative atmosphere for visiting clients. The graphic pattern on the floor offsets the rich tones of the furniture and gives the room a sharp, creative edge. Jack is always looking for new ideas, and is willing to try them out at work and home.

'My attitude from the outset has always been "yes", and I will always give something a go,' he says, 'no matter how impossible or crazy it seems at the time.'

Above and left Sketches and prototypes of Jack's jewelry designs in his studio.

Opposite Jack works at an antique desk and uses a vintage wheelchair as a seat, also bought from Mark Rochester.

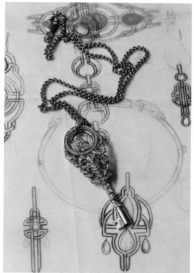

Philip Start & Brix Smith-Start

Fashion designer & stylist
Warehouse conversion | Shoreditch

Fashion designer Philip Start and his wife Brix Smith-Start, former guitarist and singer with the post-punk rock band The Fall and now a stylist and television presenter, live in a large warehouse space in the heart of Shoreditch with their two pugs, Pixie and Gladys. The location allows the couple to walk to their shops, Start and Mr Start, described by *Vogue* as two of the best fashion boutiques in the world, while the flat provides them with an incredible place for entertaining, with open-plan rooms and a huge roof terrace overlooking their fashionable corner of East London.

The couple found their home in 1999, when Brix spotted a 'for sale' sign on the side of the building while on a driving tour through the neighbourhood. At the time, Philip and Brix were living in a townhouse in Notting Hill, but they both wanted to live in a loft-style space. 'We loved the idea of a New York loft, but done in a really elegant way, with no exposed beams or wires,' Brix says, 'and being able to create a beautiful, elegant penthouse.' The flat, the last remaining one for sale in the building, was just a shell, so they engaged the services of architect and interior designer Colin Radcliffe and set to work designing the SoHo-inspired interior they had dreamed of. The work took six months to complete.

At the heart of the flat is the bespoke walnut kitchen, where the couple spend most of their time. 'I wanted a kitchen that was really easy to cook in and was a great entertaining space,' says Brix, 'and I wanted a room that does everything.' The couple throw a huge party for their friends once or twice a year, and this is when the space really comes into its own. 'People collect in the kitchen, filter upstairs and go outside. We're very informal, and energy bounces around this place in a really lovely way, so every party we've had here has been great.' Above, the open-plan entertaining space is home to Philip's art collection, and opens onto the roof terrace, which the couple have designed to feel like an extension of the interior. Philip

Opposite On the top floor, a vast living and entertaining space looks out onto a roof terrace. The black leather sofa can be re-arranged into a circle for parties.

Below The carefully curated selection of art and literature reflects Philip's passion for collecting.

'The house has a very strong sense of style and is very masculine, but there are softening feminine touches,' says Brix. 'God is in the details, and there's a particular eye in everything we bring into our house.'

Above A view from the living space into the master-bedroom suite. Brix's treasured guitar leans against the wall in the sitting room.

Opposite A photograph from Brix's time in The Fall is on display in the master bedroom.

Following pages Vintage collectibles are displayed around the home, alongside a collection of contemporary art, against a palette of white walls and wood floors.

Pages 272-73 The space has been designed so that the master bedroom and bathroom function as a private suite, which can be shut off from the rest of the flat. The bathroom has a double sink, sauna and steam room.

is a keen collector, and the space is filled with mid-century furniture and artworks by Jake and Dinos Chapman, Andy Warhol and Paula Rego. 'His greatest joy in life is buying beautiful furniture, vases and works of art,' says Brix. The flat features large expanses of exposed brick, which the couple constantly debate about whether to paint or not: 'If you paint them, it's impossible to remove, but we love the warmth of the colour.' Colour plays a vital role both at work and at home for Brix, who will often subconsciously choose clothes that reflect the colours of a favourite piece of art or an image she has seen. At one end of the apartment is the master bedroom suite, with an en suite and sauna, which can be shut off from the rest of the flat by closing the double-height doors.

It was the move to this warehouse conversion that was the catalyst for the couple to launch Start, after Brix noticed a lack of high-end fashion stores in the neighbourhood – unusually for an area that was full of design-conscious creatives. The success of Start led Philip, who started his career at the jeweller Garrard and later founded the Woodhouse chain, to launch a menswear label called Mr Start. Philip's designs echo his passion for interiors, and he has called his tailoring 'modern and architectural, defining Shoreditch luxury,' which could just as well be a description of his style at home – a home for a style-conscious couple that has been carefully edited, considered and well designed, just like a fashion collection.

Annie Morris & Idris Khan

Artists
Georgian townhouse | Islington

Above The house was built in 1760, and had been squatted for many years until the previous owner stripped it back to its bare bones. The bright-green wallpaper in the hall was brought back from the US.

Opposite Having fallen in love with the distressed look of the wood panelling and paintwork, the couple decided to leave the stairwell and several walls in their original state. The stair runner is made from a number of rag rugs sewn together.

Annie Morris and her husband Idris Khan are a stylish couple with a beautiful home to match. After studying painting at the École nationale supérieure des beaux-arts in Paris, before completing her education at the Slade School of Fine Art in London, Annie received international acclaim for her illustrations for *The Man With the Dancing Eyes*, by her good friend Sophie Dahl. She went on to be commissioned by Christopher Bailey, creative director of Burberry, to make a dress from her obsessively painted clothes pegs, which made the cover of numerous magazines. Idris, an equally successful artist, is well known for his sophisticated and complex digital collages, which have incorporated every page of the Qur'an or every Beethoven sonata, for which each sheet of music was digitally layered to become a visual representation of the composer's deafness.

Annie and Idris moved in together only three weeks after meeting, and a year later bought their Georgian townhouse in Islington, which had already had centuries of paint and wallpaper removed by the previous owner to reveal its period charm. When the couple first moved in, there was no electricity or heating, and only enough hot water for one bath a day. The couple set about completely renovating the property to make it fit for modern life, while retaining as many of its original features as possible. During the renovation process, the couple lived at the top of the house: 'It was freezing, with so many draughts,' Annie recalls.

The majority of the work was carried out on the lower ground floor, which had been a cellar and dingy bathroom. The couple transformed the space into a cosy open-plan kitchen and dining room, complete with reclaimed Aga, and turned the derelict coal vaults underneath the garden into two larders – 'the best thing we ever did,' says Annie. A small guest loo was added, and the staircase restored. After much debate, a vibrant yellow was decided upon, inspired by Monet's house in Giverny, which came from a small speck of paint that Annie's mother, herself an interior designer, had kept for years as inspiration from a previous project. The couple visited neighbouring houses to study the original cupboards and panelled detailing, before recreating them in their own home.

Upstairs, the couple have left the scraped-back paint on the woodwork as it was when they took possession of the house, adding vintage furniture and works of art, many by the couple themselves or given to them by artist friends. The first-floor sitting room and study are filled with personal touches and mementos, such as the embroidery on the sofa, hand-drawn by Annie, and Idris's photographs on the wall. On the second floor, a master bedroom and en suite provides a luxurious space for the couple to relax in, while the top floor is home to two further bedrooms. 'Our style is Charleston farmhouse-meets-modern,' says Annie. 'My theory is that if you love something, it will all go together.'

Opposite In the first-floor study, art books, sketchpads and mementos crowd together on bookshelves above an antique desk and vintage chair.

Below The couple share a studio nearby, but also use the study for work and as a quiet place for reading.

Following pages The couple's own designs are to be found throughout the house, from the freehand embroidery on the sofa to the artwork on the walls.

Above and left Packaging from around the world that caught Annie's eye on her travels forms an unusual display in the larder. The colour of the kitchen was matched from a speck of paint that Annie's mother, an interior decorator, had kept for years.

Opposite Antique chairs are pulled up to the farmhouse table in the lower ground-floor kitchen. The couple visited neighbouring houses to recreate the original details of the house.

Right and below Idris designed
the en-suite bathroom, with
its romantic roll-top bath. The
original wood and paintwork
can be glimpsed behind the
bathroom mirror.

Opposite Crisp white linen on
the bed creates a beautiful contrast
to the scraped-back wood panels
in one of the top-floor bedrooms.

'I don't want the house to be precious, so artworks
come and go. It's constantly changing and that
makes it exciting, although it's nice to be settled,'
says Annie. 'We always laugh and say what on
earth will we talk about, once the house is done?'

Kyle & Jo Stewart

Designers
Victorian terraced house | Columbia Road

Above The bright colours and graphic shapes in the couple's home were heavily influenced by their frequent travels abroad for work.

Opposite The stark white colour scheme of the kitchen is punctuated by a bespoke splashback in bright yellow and bright accessories.

Kyle and Jo Stewart, owners of the hip lifestyle and fashion store Goodhood, located in the even hipper neighbourhood of Hoxton, both trained in fashion and met while they were working for denim brand Levi's. The couple then worked for Nike in Amsterdam, before returning to London to set up Goodhood. Having lived, worked and travelled extensively throughout Europe and the United States, as well as Japan, Kyle and Jo have an international perspective on design, and have consolidated their experiences to create a fresh, dynamic home for themselves and their baby son, filled with things they love.

Overlooking a pretty green near Columbia Road flower market, their two-bedroom Victorian terraced house is in a conservation area close to the bustle of Brick Lane and Shoreditch. After living in the world's most exciting cities, this neighbourhood in Hackney seemed the obvious place to settle. 'We liked the creative vibe of the area, having been living in New York,' says Jo. 'We used to go out near here and always really liked it. We also liked the proximity to the centre of London, and the fact that when you're in your own house, it's very quiet, like being in a small village.'

The house's previous owners had carried out some renovations, but the kitchen was shabby and freestanding, so it was replaced with sleek, white fitted units and a bespoke glass splashback, setting the tone for the rest of the house. The couple added a wall next to the stairs in the open-plan living room, and completely remodelled the first floor of the house in stages, replacing the bathroom, changing all the doors and adding custom-designed storage. 'I love doing interiors, and do all the technical drawings and measurements myself,' Jo says.

Upstairs the couple introduced floor-to-ceiling sliding doors to connect the rooms. 'Japanese style has hugely influenced our own style at home,

Opposite A dining table and chairs take up one corner of the open-plan living space, which leads to the kitchen. The couple found the table base and had it powder-coated, adding a bespoke extendable top from Unto This Last.

Below In the same room, a shelving unit doubles as a compact office. Jo designed the Missoni-inspired fabric on the vintage chairs especially for the space.

because it's so visual,' says Jo. Travels around Japan also influenced the couple's choice of colours, from the monochrome palette and wood tones to the bright graphic pops of colour often seen in Japanese advertising. Even though their home is sharply graphic in design, Kyle and Jo still wanted it to be calm and relaxing, and chose comfortable furniture and textiles, along with lots of wood. In the bedroom, bespoke storage is hidden behind panels of laser-cut wood, and the choice of natural fabrics such as cotton, linen or wool for upholstery and textiles continues the feeling of relaxed comfort. 'There's a lot of collected stuff, things that we like,' says Kyle. 'We try to collect nice things that are classic or future classics, a mixture of old and new.'

Following pages The wall behind the bed is painted black to showcase artwork by Kyle. Opposite the bed, the picture of Kate Moss was a gift from a friend who had worked on the advertising campaign.

Left and below Collectible toys and urban street art give the nursery cool style credentials. Jo found the Burger King sign on Brick Lane and turned a vintage kitchen cabinet into funky storage.

Opposite Diner chairs from the 1950s, bought in Amsterdam, hang on the wall in the stairwell and are brought down when friends come to dinner.

Fashion designer
Victorian conversion flat | Dalston

Ally Capellino, who launched her first collection in 1980, is the designer of enduringly popular leather accessories and handbags, toted by some of London's most fashion-forward trendsetters. Having lived in various East End locations over the years, she now lives with her two children in a bright and airy Victorian conversion in Dalston. It was the 'upside-down' layout of the flat – with the sitting room and kitchen on the upper ground floor, and the bedrooms and bathrooms on the floor below – that first attracted her to it, along with the high ceilings and abundance of natural light.

Ally immediately set about making the space her own, painting the doors and skirting boards black and laying wood floors throughout, which she also painted black in the sitting room and kitchen. 'I wanted it to have a feeling of light and space, but at the same time be homely and comfortable,' she says. 'I'm not very good at chucking anything away, so inevitably it's more messy than I'd like!' Double glass doors were added at the rear of the kitchen, overlooking the garden, along with a balcony so that she and the children could enjoy breakfast on the sunny terrace. The glass doors allow even more light to flood into the room, which also has floor-to-ceiling windows at both ends. Well known for her use of durable yet beautiful materials in her handbag designs, Ally's home reflects her simple, pared-back aesthetic. A huge wooden table, which had a former life as a counter

Above A corner of the open-plan sitting room and kitchen is given over to a compact workspace, with an Eames chair design and functional desk.

Below Items collected by Ally and the children are displayed in front of the fireplace and on the coffee table.

top in her Wardour Street shop, now has pride of place in the kitchen. 'It slides around on some old Habitat trestles, but we can get up to about twenty people around it,' she says. 'It's a lovely piece of very heavy oak.'

When Ally first moved into the house, the lower ground floor had just two rooms, which she describes as 'dreary'. To these she added en-suite bathrooms, creating restful bedroom suites for herself and the children that open out to the large garden with its fruit trees and flowering shrubs. Her own bedroom is decorated simply, with an orange monk's habit functioning as a colourful bedspread, and her bathroom is lined with bright-yellow tiles, both colours that feature heavily in her collections. 'I'm a bit of a hippy, I suppose,' she says, 'and I love to be surrounded by things that I've picked up on travels, or have been given to me, and that hold some nice memories.'

Robert Polidori AFTER THE FLOOD

Above A monk's habit provides an injection of bright colour in Ally's bedroom on the lower ground floor.

Opposite In the sitting room above, an industrial lamp hangs over a bright-green sofa and a coffee table made from reclaimed wood.

Ally describes her home as a work in progress. 'I'm lucky enough to be in a job where visual stimulation is part of my research,' she explains, 'and so it is something that's always feeding me.' The most important thing to her when decorating is that the objects she brings home have meaning and are connected to the people and places she loves. 'I don't shop for anything, I'm a complete impulse buyer. I went shopping recently because all our cushions had fallen to pieces, but I didn't see anything to connect with. Then my son and his girlfriend bought some wacko fabric in the market, and made up some cushions for my birthday. I don't know how well they go, but they have a story and a link to something important, so they work.'

Graham & Jo
Atkins-Hughes

Photographer & stylist
Victorian terraced house | Hackney

They say you need to decorate three houses before you get it right, and Graham and Jo Atkins-Hughes have certainly nailed it with their third home, a huge Victorian terraced house in Dalston. The couple had been living in nearby Stoke Newington, but their search brought them eastwards because of the scale of the houses. Decorated in sensuous dark, inky hues and furnished with vintage finds, the house has been a popular location for film and fashion shoots for more than ten years.

Jo, a fashion stylist, and Graham, who trained under Bruce Weber and Annie Liebowitz and is now a successful interiors and fashion photographer in his own right, married within three months of meeting. Having found the perfect partner, finding the ideal home took a little longer as they were searching for a place that would also make a good location site. Before the couple bought the house in 2001, four families had been living in it, so it was in need of some restoration, but most of the original features were in place. Graham and Jo knew that they wanted plenty of expansive rooms, so they set about removing walls on each floor, creating an

Above Red-gloss units look dramatic against the dark walls in the kitchen. In the garden, the walls are painted the same colour as the interior to give a feeling of continuity.

Opposite Deep-green walls and black stairs form a striking contrast to the vintage glass chandelier in the entrance hall.

Above A collection of ceramic vases in earthy tones is lined up on the mantelpiece in the sitting room, and a vintage chair has been re-upholstered in lush green velvet.

Opposite Jo found the velvet modular sofa on eBay, which, luckily, fitted as though it had been made for the room. The walls are painted in Downpipe by Farrow & Ball.

Following pages Richly coloured textiles and wood tones are an effective combination against the dark walls and floors in the first-floor sitting room.

open-plan kitchen and living space on the lower ground floor, a double sitting room above, and a luxurious master bedroom suite on the first floor, leaving two rooms at the top for an office and second bedroom. While most of the period features remained, additional cornicing and fireplaces were made for the sitting room and master bedroom to replicate what would originally have been there. The fireplace in the bedroom soon had to be taken out again, however, to make way for the huge bank of built-in storage that now absorbs the sound of noisy neighbours, which had been echoing down the chimney. With her knack for finding a bargain and making it look a million dollars, Jo found the two bedroom chairs by the side of the road, and spotted the four design-classic dining chairs outside a charity shop.

The couple knew that, in contrast to other location houses, they wanted to decorate their home in dark colours. Although it was a risk, Jo wanted the house to be a comfortable home, as well as a successful business. 'We've gradually gone darker with each house we've lived in,' she says. 'I've never had a white or cream house – the first was navy and cornflower blue, the second chocolate brown and sludgy green, and now it is almost black.' Now that the couple have two young sons, the house is also a well-loved family home, and the dark colour scheme has come into its own as a more practical option than the pristine white interiors of other location houses. This is definitely a family converted to the dark side.

Right and below Works of art
stand out against the elegantly
muted colour scheme.

Opposite Jo's office is designated
by a vintage desk and chair.
Elsewhere in the house, treasured
objects are displayed on antique
sideboards and tables.

Following pages Bespoke storage
in the master bedroom blocks
out noise from the neighbours.
The chairs were a lucky find
on the street, and re-upholstered
in yellow velvet.

'The house feels very warm, comfortable and cosy,
and works really well with colour,' Jo explains.
'We've used lots of warm colours, and people
bring everything from bright to sludgy hues for
shoots. They all look great against the dark walls.'

and
Pioneers

Georg
Baselitz

HELMUT NEWTON

A
GUN
FOR
HIRE

WORLDS
AND
WINDOWS
BY
GILBERT
AND
GEORGE

The Day of
the Peacock
Style for Men
1963–1973

mead

notebook

A Photographer's Life

DEN
NO
PP
IS
ER
H

O U
U O
T F
T X
H
E
S
I
I
X
E
T
S
I
E
S

POSTCARDS FROM THE BOYS
RINGO STARR

BLACK
ORPHEUS

STUDIO
FILM
CLUB

PETER DOIG

Opposite In Jo Berryman's sitting room, art books are placed on shelves with the cover artwork on display.

Graham Atkins-Hughes [302]
Location 78
+44 (0)20 7275 0004
bookings@location78.com
location78.com
+44 (0)7850 279 802
graham@grahamatkinshughes.com
grahamatkinshughes.com

Jo Atkins-Hughes [302]
+44 (0)7718 885 446
jo@location78.com
joatkinshughes.com

Jo Berryman [108]
Matrushka
4 Willoughby Road, London NW3 1SA
+44 (0)207 435 1386
info@matrushka.co.uk
matrushka.co.uk

Eelke Jan Bles [242]
Solid Floor
61 Paddington Street, London W1U 4JD
+44 (0)20 7486 4838
marylebone@solidfloor.co.uk
53 Pembridge Road, London W11 3HG
+44 (0)20 7221 9166
nottinghill@solidfloor.co.uk
solidfloor.co.uk
Solid ID
273 Fulham Road, London SW10 9PZ
+44 (0)20 7351 3045
showroom@solidid.co.uk
solidid.co.uk

Ally Capellino [296]
Shops:
9 Calvert Avenue, London E2 7JP
+44 (0)20 7033 7843
312 Portobello Road, London W10 5RU
+44 (0)20 8964 1022
shop@allycapellino.co.uk
allycapellino.co.uk

Priscilla Carluccio [72]
info@priscilla-carluccio.com
priscilla-carluccio.com

David Carter [216]
Boutique hotel:
40 Winks
109 Mile End Road, London E1 4UJ
+44 (0)20 7790 0259
reservations@40winks.org
40winks.org
info@alacarter.com
alacarter.com

Sebastian Conran [118]
Studio:
2 Munden Street, London W14 0RH
+44 (0)20 7036 0636
studio@sebastianconran.com
sebastianconran.com

Marianne Cotterill [26]
+44 (0)7917 788 969
info@mapesburyroad.com
mapesburyroad.com
marianne@mariannecotterill.com
mariannecotterill.com

Neisha Crosland [126]
+44 (0)20 7657 1150
info@neishacrosland.com
neishacrosland.com

Robin Derrick [36]
robin.derrick@mac.com
robinderrick.tumblr.com

Rory Dobner [136]
+44 (0)7775 212 425
enquiries@rorydobner.com
rorydobner.com

James-Lee Duffy [62]
+44 (0)7792 695 571
info@weareshadows.com
weareshadows.com

Claire Durbridge [92]
clairedurbridge.com

Jack du Rose [258]
+44 (0)20 7503 7064
uk@durosefinejewellery.com
us@durosefinejewellery.com
durosefinejewellery.com

Chris Dyson [180]
Office:
11 Princelet Street, London E1 6QH
+44 (0)20 7247 1816
info@chrisdyson.co.uk
chrisdyson.co.uk

Lisa Eldridge [36]
lisaeldridge.com

Martin Firrell [46]
firstcontact@martinfirrell.com
martinfirrell.com

Laura Ford & Andrew Sabin [100]
andrew.sabin@blueyonder.co.uk
andrewsabin.org

Kate Halfpenny [62]
Showroom:
104 Camden Mews, London NW1 9AG
+44 (0)7976 761 166
dresses@halfpennylondon.com
halfpennylondon.com

Graham Judkins [86]
+44 (0)20 7289 8059
info@untitleddesignstudio.com
untitleddesignstudio.com

Mawi Keivom [208]
Shop:
11 Calvert Avenue, London E2 7JP
+44 (0)20 7033 9853
shop@mawi.co.uk
mawi.co.uk

Alex Lewis [226]
Studio:
Top floor, 9 Beatty Road, London N16 8EA
+44 (0)7710 102 917
alex@alexlewis.co.uk
alexlewis.co.uk

Annie Morris & Idris Khan [274]
info@anniemorris.com
anniemorris.com

Adriana Natcheva [18]
Office:
6 Kensington Court Mews,
London W8 5DR
+44 (0)20 7937 7772
info@grovesnatcheva.com
grovesnatcheva.com

Marc Newson [54]
Studio:
7 Howick Place, London SW1P 1BB
+44 (0)20 7932 0990
pod@marc-newson.com
marc-newson.com

Zandra Rhodes [232]
Salon:
79 Bermondsey Street, London SE1 3XF
+44 (0)20 7403 5333
zandrarhodes.com

James Russell & Hannah Plumb [78]
+44 (0)20 7738 5547
us@jamesplumb.co.uk
jamesplumb.co.uk

Bob Sakoui [92]
+44 (0) 207 112 8337
info@distinguishedandco.com
distinguishedandco.com

Margo Selby [146]
Studio:
Bradstowe House, 35 Middle Wall,
Whitstable, Kent CT5 1BF
info@margoselby.com
margoselby.com

Pippa Small [166]
Shop:
201 Westbourne Grove,
London W11 2SB
+44 (0)20 7792 1292
shop@pippasmall.com
pippasmall.com

Michael Smythe [200]
michael@nomad.org.uk
nomad.org.uk

Philip Start & Brix Smith-Start [264]
Shops:
42–44 Rivington Street, London EC2A 3QP
+44 (0)20 7729 3334
womens@start-london.com
59 Rivington Street, London EC2A 3QQ
+44 (0)20 7739 3636
mens@start-london.com
40 Rivington Street, London EC2A 3LX
+44 (0)20 7729 6272
tailoring@start-london.com
start-london.com

Kyle & Jo Stewart [286]
Goodhood
41 Coronet Street, London N1 6HD
+44 (0)20 7729 3600
store@goodhood.co.uk
goodhoodstore.com

Charlotte Stockdale [54]
i-D
124 Tabernacle Street, London EC2A 4SA
+44 (0)20 7490 9710
i-donline.com

Joelle Talmasse & Martyn Gayle [152]
97 St Ervans Road, London W10 5QY
info@breaad.com
breaad.com

Jo Wood [158]
info@jowoodorganics.com
jowoodorganics.com

Acknowledgments

When we first set out to photograph the homes of London's creative community, we embarked on an exciting and inspirational journey alongside some of the city's most creative residents. We would like to thank everyone who allowed us to document how they express themselves in that most personal of spaces, their homes. None of this would have been possible without the trust, patience and generosity of those who have taken part.

About the author

Emily Wheeler is a stylist, writer and interior designer. Since graduating from the KLC School of Design, London, she has written about interiors for the *Telegraph*, *Mail on Sunday*, *Sunday Times Style* and *Easy Living* magazine, as well as several international publications. She contributes regularly to her own lifestyle and interiors blog.

About the photographer

Ingrid Rasmussen is a travel and interiors photographer whose previous titles for Thames & Hudson include *New Country Style: England*, *New London Style* and four titles from the *StyleCity* series. Her work has appeared in Conde Nast Traveller, *Vogue*, *The Sunday Times*, *Elle Decoration*, the *Telegraph Magazine* and the *Guardian*. She lives in London.